Self Help Mindset

3 Books in 1:

Anger Management,

Depression and Anxiety Therapy,

Self-Love

Howard Patel

Self Help Mindset

Written by Howard Patel

First Edition

Copyrights Notice

Limited Liability

Please note that the content of this book is based on personal experience and various information sources.

Although the author has made every effort to present accurate, up-to-date, reliable, and complete information in this book, they make no representations or warranties concerning the accuracy or completeness of the content of this book and specifically disclaim any implied warranties of merchantability or fitness for a particular purpose.

Your particular circumstances may not be suited to the example illustrated in this book; in fact, they likely will not be. You should use the information in this book at your own risk.

All trademarks, service marks, product names, and the characteristics of any names mentioned in this book are considered the property of their respective owners and are used only for reference. No endorsement is implied when we use one of these terms.

This book is only for personal use. Please note the information contained within this document is for educational and entertainment purposes only and no warranties of any kind are declared or implied. Readers acknowledge that the author is not engaged in providing any kind of medical, dietary, nutritional, psychological, psychiatric advice, nor professional medical advice.

Please consult a doctor, before attempting any techniques outlined in this book. Nothing in this book is intended to replace common sense or medical consultation or professional advice and is meant only to inform. By reading this book, the reader agrees that under no circumstances is the author responsible for any losses, direct or indirect, which are incurred as a result of the use of the information contained within this document, including, but not limited to, errors, omissions, or inaccuracies.

page intentionally left blank

Anger Management

How to Master Your Anger, Control Your Emotions And Find Joy In Life

Howard Patel

Anger Management

Written by Howard Patel

First Edition

Copyrights Notice

Limited Liability

Please note that the content of this book is based on personal experience and various information sources.

Although the author has made every effort to present accurate, up-to-date, reliable, and complete information in this book, they make no representations or warranties concerning the accuracy or completeness of the content of this book and specifically disclaim any implied warranties of merchantability or fitness for a particular purpose.

Your particular circumstances may not be suited to the example illustrated in this book; in fact, they likely will not be. You should use the information in this book at your own risk.

All trademarks, service marks, product names, and the characteristics of any names mentioned in this book are considered the property of their respective owners and are used only for reference. No endorsement is implied when we use one of these terms.

This book is only for personal use. Please note the information contained within this document is for educational and entertainment purposes only and no warranties of any kind are declared or implied. Readers acknowledge that the author is not engaged in providing any kind of medical, dietary, nutritional, psychological, psychiatric advice, nor professional medical advice.

Please consult a doctor, before attempting any techniques outlined in this book. Nothing in this book is intended to replace common sense or medical consultation or professional advice and is meant only to inform. By reading this book, the reader agrees that under no circumstances is the author responsible for any losses, direct or indirect, which are incurred as a result of the use of the information contained within this document, including, but not limited to, errors, omissions, or inaccuracies.

Table of Contents

Introduction

Anger is an expression of hostility in reaction to dissatisfaction. The dissatisfaction can stem from a variety of sources; a reaction to bad news you received, something that was done to you or you perceive was done to you, an argument you had, or even just your perception of things and people in your life; even depending on your mood to start with, something as quick as another driver cutting you off, or a cashier giving you back the wrong change can trigger anger.

We've all gotten angry over large and small issues, and overreacted to bad news or something annoying. The expression of anger becomes an issue when we cross the line from a simple expression of dissatisfaction to a consistent overreaction that harms ourselves and people around us emotionally, psychologically, or even physically.

Can Anger Be Appropriate?

Yes. Anger is one way of expressing that you don't like how you've been treated, letting another person know, I want this fixed and made right, or you're upset about something.

Expressing anger lets someone know, this is somewhat serious, at least to me. This needs attention and resolution if possible.

People would be surprised if you didn't get angry over some things. Anger is a normal emotion and part of every day with its purpose and proper time.

You could get angry over losing your job, if someone stole something from you, if your car broke down, when a partner breaks up with you, arguing with a family member when you feel like someone's not giving you enough respect, or your fair due. These are just a few examples of when people would expect you to get angry and you'd have a right to. Various causes and reasons can trigger anger. It happens to us all. It's perfectly normal, up to a point, and within moderation.

Sometimes you need to express anger before you can begin to resolve an issue, especially if it involves someone else who thus far hasn't considered your side of the issue.

Can You Use Anger Constructively?

Anger expresses dissatisfaction. You can use anger constructively to make your feelings clear and express a need to resolve an issue.

If someone cuts you in line at the coffee shop every morning, you can get angry, letting them know you don't like being cut. They might acknowledge it and back off the following morning and let you go first. You've expressed your dissatisfaction and resolved the conflict.

You feel like your parents never listen to you. You might get angry during a discussion or argument. They might wonder why you're so angry and ask why.

Then you can explain your feelings, you feel like they never listen to you. It hurts your feelings and your self-esteem. Who hasn't blurted something out in a heated family argument?

As long as it's not an intentionally insulting, hurtful comment, "you're stupid", "you don't care", then you're expressing your feelings toward resolving a conflict. Your parents will make more of an effort to listen the next time you argue.

Anger can be used to define boundaries. The person at the coffee shop knows you don't like being cut.

You could get angry if someone slaps you on the back unexpectedly. They'll know you don't like that and hopefully won't do it again.

Some people get angry when you talk to them while they're reading. Some people get angry if you sit too close to them.

They're expressing a need for boundaries, as long as they're not insulting or hurtful.

You can use anger constructively to express concern over how someone is treating you.

If you shout, "get off my back," while someone's asking you for something, you're expressing anxiety, telling them, please, not right now. You might be too brief, and hopefully, later you'll make time to discuss it further, calmly and politely, but you've expressed concern or stated a need through anger.

Anger can be a constructive way to simply vent, or cathartic, blow off steam, provided you're not mistreating someone in the process. You might kick a rock when you're tired from gardening. You might stamp your mouse if your computer freezes.

Provided you don't break something or hurt someone, we all need to blow off steam sometimes.

You should consider whether you have an anger control issue if you break things regularly, or if you hurt someone's feelings, or even hurt someone physically.

Like you can express boundaries through anger, you can express preferences in behavior or routines. "Do you have to do that now?", "Why is it always after lunchtime?" are expressions of anger that let someone know you'd prefer they did or said something at a different time, find a new routine you're both happy with. Again, discuss it more when you're calm.

Angry commands can become a form of control and abuse. Anger can be used constructively for various purposes if it's not taken too far or used too often.

How Can Anger Control You?

Anger can control you in a variety of ways, psychologically, emotionally, even physically, and can control how you handle people or situations, even how little problems escalate into big problems.

You can get so angry that all you think about is how to retaliate for a perceived wrong. You're in a psychological frame of mind to do damage and seek payback or revenge, not resolve a conflict for both parties' sake.

After a few bad fights with someone, you might decide you just can't get along with that person. Your anger has made you decide it is pointless to try. That's one more bridge you've burned because you couldn't work through your anger to repair the relationship.

Too many angry fits and your personality may begin to change. You might start to become an "angry person", quick to anger, upset more often than not.

Your total outlook might change for the worse. You might become pessimistic or cynical when previously you were usually hopeful and optimistic. Once you're becoming pessimistic, you'll behave differently. When previously you might try something new, now you might think, why bother, or, I'm bound to fail, so why try at all?

As you might adopt a negative attitude about new things and situations, you might adopt negative attitudes about people too, new people you meet, and even people you already know. Why should I ask my wife to go out? She'll only say no.

Why bother asking my son to play basketball? He's only going to beat me again. When your outlook about people becomes negative, then how you treat them will change too.

You could find yourself being more critical of your wife or your son or whoever you're developing new negative attitudes about.

As your perspective about the person or situation changes, so can the way you deal with him or them. You might have made the best of it before. Now you think, what's the point? Whatever happens, happens.

You can begin to approach everything with a negative perspective, assume the worst from the start, and assume there's no point trying to improve something, a situation, a relationship.

People around you will begin to feed off or react to your negative perspective. They might talk to you less. They might try less to work things out with you. They might fight more often with you.

You can begin a downward spiral that gets worse and worse until anger and a negative outlook can turn into depression and feelings of hopelessness. You might lose touch with people who used to be close to you. As you stop trying, they stop trying, until one day they decide there's no point knowing you at all.

Chapter 1

Understanding of Anger

Anger may be completely ugly. With the misery and suffering it causes, you will have firsthand experience. Its poisonous impacts have been minimized in many aspects of life. Anger will wreck connections. This will raise the likelihood of heart problems. And it is just plain uncomfortable to have a life filled with anger.

You might not be confident that when you're mad, you should change the way you behave. But we agree you will, and we thank you for having picked up this book and explored the role of anger in your life. This is a huge step in leading a life that is more peaceful and prosperous.

When they're upset, it's very normal for people to respond strongly. People of all genders, levels of schooling, racial origins, and types of income do it.

We offer tales of individuals that have suffered from frustration in a wide variety of circumstances in this novel. All the stories have in common is that anger has gotten in the way of the desire to deal with the problems of life successfully.

This chapter aims to answer some simple anger questions, include reliable statistics, and present an information base that you can build on when you move forward with your goal of changing your actions while you are angry.

We will help you make sense of the many components of anger, and we are going to answer common questions about it. And you will have to ask yourself this simple question at some point: "Is my anger helpful?"

Anger can be hard to grasp. In reality, you may have both felt satisfied and sad after the frustration you shared. You will possibly remember several occasions, for instance, when your frustration seems warranted, almost right.

"If you're like other people, you may have said to yourself," I'm entitled to be furious at what she did! "Nevertheless, if you are honest with yourself, you can accept that there have been times when your frustration was too intense, too long, needless issues created, or just plain foolish.

You could remember occasions when your irritation leads to fights, headaches, regrets, foolish actions, and other concerns, including when you felt it was acceptable.

One of our fundamental emotions is frustration. Scholars have written about frustration in people of all ages, and from all parts of the globe.

Some aspects of dissatisfaction are optimistic. It's part of relationships' ups and downs and can be a positive indication that something isn't right.

Any anger may also increase empathy between individuals. Your voice raised in anger, for instance, will indicate to people that you are talking about something important, and it will cause them to listen to you more closely.

Or anger will encourage you to make progress in your life and even face challenges that you've been avoiding. Zest, enthusiasm, and passion may also result from frustration.

The plain truth is that in a world without anger, we wouldn't want to exist. It has its advantages, and so this book isn't about removing anger from your life altogether.

But frustration can lead to severe damage and suffering as well. A typical effect of frustration is a disruption to ties with family members, acquaintances, and co-workers.

Angry people don't think straight, and the wrong choices are made. Furthermore, long-term frustration, such as heart disease and stroke, may cause significant medical complications. There are just a couple of the reasons for holding your frustration in place. If you read on, we'll send you some.

Anger is an intense reaction you are knowingly having. Anger is an internal perception of arousal at its heart, followed by individual emotions, perceptions, and desires.

What Causes Anger?

There are, in fact, many different triggers of anger. This is why, on TV, in newspapers, on the radio, and on the internet, you see experts sharing such different viewpoints. Let's start with an interpretation that brings together what most practitioners who research and treat anger accept:

Anger is an irrational response to others' unwelcome and sometimes unforeseen behavior. It arises based on the potential danger to physical wellbeing, possessions, personal appearance, sense of equality, or rational comfort wish.

How people portray frustration depends on where they are and whether it has worked for them in the past to communicate frustration.

First of all, this very formal definition applies to what we term an immediate cause: something negative happens (such as finding that a friend has been gossiping about you), and you react instantly with indignation.

You fault the other person for the way you behave when you're upset. This is considered a stimulus to reaction sequence by psychologists. The stimulation is the gossiping of your friend about you; your indignation is the answer. We will discuss some causes of anger;

- Learning
- Thinking
- Human nature

Learning

A lot of the irritation stems from patterns you've built over the years. Although there's always an instant trigger that gets you rolling, you've spent a long time learning when and how to get mad.

Sometimes, learning requires what psychologists call simulation. This suggests learning by watching what happens (in other words, learning by example) to other people as they get upset.

People tend to mimic others' actions, especially when they assume that specific actions create good outcomes. To list only a few examples, learning through modeling will come by watching the angry action of friends, colleagues, or characters on TV, in movies, and in video games.

In this way, there are a lot of ways to think about frustration. Then you take what you've heard about anger to turn it into your laws, such as, "When people insult me or gossip about me, I'm going to get mad to scream." That is me, and I do that! Not all angry behavior, of course, comes from watching people.

You have your distinctive, unique impressions and tradition of learning. Your history of learning consists of two sections, which are considered reinforcement and punishment by psychologists.

Although you usually don't think anything about it, repercussions accompany any of your actions. You prefer to replicate conduct that results in an outcome you like.

For starters, if you scream at your son to clean his room and he does it, the next time you ask him to clean his room, you are more likely to call at him again. Conduct that is enhanced (yelling at your son) in the short term becomes a long-term habit.

In comparison, the action is often accompanied by a result that you don't like. For starters, if you aggressively demand strangers to be quiet in a movie theatre, then they swear at you, a reaction that leads to a loud, then unpleasant argument, you are less likely to tell strangers to be quiet in the future.

Conduct that is punished in the short term should not become a habit (telling strangers to be quiet). Reinforcements and punishments powerfully form your patterns over time.

When you're mad, the way you behave now has a lot to do with the repercussions of your past mad conduct.

Thinking

Anyways of thought trigger frustration as well. You can misunderstand or misrepresent what other individuals do or say, for instance. You may be exaggerating, turning small issues into significant deals.

Or your opinions can be challenging and inflexible. You probably believe the following suggestions when angry:

- You've been forgotten, overlooked, or poorly punished.
- Somebody else has behaved incorrectly.
- If he/she had wanted to, the person who angered you might have behaved differently.
- The person who offended you ought to have behaved better.

Your assumptions about others' actions may or may not be valid.

There may be times where you have been wrong about other people's motivations. Perhaps the friend who is not answering your calls or responding to your messages struggles with personal or family member health issues. Job assignments can be overwhelmed by the future deadline that keeps holding you off.

Or maybe it was late for your teenage daughter, who is expected to be home by dinner time when she stopped at the mall to get you a birthday present. She wouldn't want to tell you that and spoil the surprise.

You don't actively analyze your thinking about poor treatment at others' hands, whether you're like most individuals. It only seems that your feelings arrive naturally.

However, unfortunately, the assumptions will become skewed, unreliable, and inflated over time. It is your thought, in that sense, which triggers your anger.

We'll return to this theory and teach you how to analyze and alter the exaggerated and skewed pieces of your mind.

Human Nature

Anger turned out to be part of human nature. In nonhuman species, anger may still occur, and the reasons for angry and violent actions in other species are equivalent to our motives for such activities.

For instance, monkeys display anger when they threaten their territories and when other monkeys attempt to take their food or mate with their partners. When they're mad, other animals do stuff to make themselves look large and stable.

These behaviors include making their bodies appear larger, standing, hissing, growling, biting, kicking, and scraping on their hind legs. Such activity is like a lot of our own. It is a warning to stay away as animals growl or hiss.

Our yelling sounds much like their growling. When animals stand straight and get larger, they say they're too powerful to mess with.

That's equivalent to waving a hand in a provocative stance or bending forward.

When we feel challenged, anger comes out, and it worked with ancient humans. Around the same time, just an inclination or an impulse to behave with frustration is implicated with our resemblance to other species.

We can conquer these impulses as individuals who are often influenced by thought, affirmation, communities, classes, and community.

What is Aggression?

There is always a misunderstanding between anger and its cousin, hostility. Anger is an emotion that you experience mainly inside. Aggression is a behavior that may be witnessed by anyone.

Usually, violent conduct towards other people is seen, which involves throwing objects, pushing, shoving, punching, etc. Sneaky, indirect acts, such as scraping someone's car or removing office equipment from a co-worker you do not like, are also included.

Offensive conduct varies from comparatively mild to extreme (assault and murder) (a teen who throws a school mate in frustration). When we say that specific violence is minor, we don't intend to display that identifying and analyzing it is unnecessary.

Intentionally offensive actions aimed towards another person is almost always inappropriate. Nonetheless, multiple violent acts can have various harmful effects. In contrast to being struck in the chest, being hit by a hurled pencil at school is minor.

Aggression often entails the intent factor. The conduct may have been purposely carried out for you to classify the behavior of your partner, wife, or child (or of an acquaintance, stranger, or co-worker) as hostile.

Usually, we should not perceive dentists or physical therapists as aggressive, even if any acute discomfort can be induced. The statute treats intentional and accidental offenses as somewhat distinct.

Deliberate violence is treated even more harshly than accidental violence, like where an individual is injured in an automobile crash, like where crime is anticipated.

Likewise, a friend's deliberate bad conduct is much more important than his or her unintended behavior. You'd be smart to determine whether or not their acts were intentional if you're questioning the adverse conduct of people in your life.

Does Anger Cause Aggression?

The fuel for violence is often anger. However, most frequently, anger arises without provocation. And violent actions often occur without frustration. For instance, hunters are aggressive-their aim to kill animals, but they do not harbor resentment towards those animals.

Aggression with Anger

You may think anger and violence are like conjoined twins if you read the papers. An angered man beats his mother after an argument; an angry employee threatens a boss after not getting a rise, an angry youth shoots his teachers or friends after he is ignored or mistaken. You also hear about passion crimes.

Yet the real picture of the relationship between anger and violence is blurred by these high-profile events.

Some people indeed have good associations between their frustration, and aggression-they believe it's OK to be offensive when they're mad.

And a lot of the abuse that we witness and read about on the television is due to anger, which makes anger and provocation seem like they all happen together.

But really, it is the case, not the norm. The reality is, less than 10 percent of the time, deliberate physical violence accompanies frustration. Anger happens on its own most of the time, and it's anger itself that is the right challenge for most people.

This suggests that anger reveals itself only as shouting, complaining, verbally demeaning, frowning, being in a bad mood, or pouting, 90 percent of the time, not as violence.

Especially if one person assaults another (an upset adult, for instance, says, "I'm going to let you have it!"), violence normally does not accompany anger.

By this, we say that there are no physical acts associated with shouting and complaining that are measurable. Nevertheless, the value of the relationship between anger and violence we don't want to downplay.

Aggression is often accompanied by anger, as when the arousal and physical excitement of anger is accompanied by feelings of retaliation and malicious behavior.

Nevertheless, regardless of whether it is accompanied by violence, anger is a significant issue in its own right.

Aggression without Anger

Without anger, violence, and damage to other humans may also happen. For starters, in one case, a New York teenager thoughtlessly dropped a frozen turkey into a passing car from a highway overpass, and a driver was seriously injured.

But the teen wasn't upset at the driver. He had no idea that his thoughtless behavior could have harmed anyone. Or occasionally, not out of anger, adolescents and adults act violently as part of a scheme to rob from others.

A purse snatcher can hurt the victim's arm and, during the robbery, throw her to the ground. The attacker is not furious at the survivor.

The aim is clearly to get her purse stolen.

Check If Your Anger is Normal?

You may question if your anger pattern is natural. One way to address this question is to ask whether, when you get upset, things in your life usually change or get worse.

The other way of handling this question is to understand your anger's frequency, severity, and length.

- **How much do you get angry?** In a survey we took of adults living in the city, we found that about 25 percent of individuals were angry one or two days per week. Almost every day, some of our study subjects mentioned feeling upset. A variety of issues, such as poor self-image, loneliness, shame, weaker relationships with friends and family members, headaches and other medical problems, and legal troubles, tended to go along with being angry. Another 25 percent of our test subjects indicated that they seldom, if ever, became upset. With far fewer family, medical, and legal concerns, these individuals tended to have far happier lives.
- **How intense is your anger?** A mild to moderate strength of feeling is included in the frustration we call natural. The more severe your irritation is, the more likely it is for you to create problems. Mild and Mild in the lives of most people, frustration does not cause significant damage to Individuals.
- **How long would the indignation last?** Some persons waste days, weeks, or months at others' mercy, focusing on past

unfairness and crappy care. For long times, being angry interferes with getting on with life and with feeling pleasure and satisfaction.

Think of any of the moments when you've been nuts. Have you been wondering about it? Whether your anger was too weak, too intense, or was it, just right? Does the discontent arise too often?

Will it last long enough? While sometimes anger can be a Yeah, you have to closely examine your life to determine whether it's helping or hurting you.

If Men Get Angrier Than Women

Differences between men and women have to do with another common issue. Some people think that men are angrier and more volatile than women are.

Anger, though, tends to be an experience of equal opportunities, because the fact is that men and women are much more similar than they are different.

A few psychologists have also noticed that, more often than men, women get angry. From a large-scale study of experimental findings, for example, John Archer suggests that women are marginally more likely to get angry and use physical violence than men.

Of course, as men are usually heavier, they inflict more harm when they attack women. In our personal experience, both men and women have a lot of resentment.

For the same reasons, both sexes tend to get angry with almost equal frequency, and they perceive and articulate themselves in standard ways. So, you're certainly not alone, whether you're a woman or a man.

Chapter 2

Anger Management

Anger management aims to minimize the psychological arousal and emotions caused by anger. A person can't avoid or rid him or herself of the people or things that cause him or her to get angry, nor can he or she change them; however, he or she can learn to control his or her reactions.

Certain psychological tests are used to measure the strength or intensity of feeling of anger, how prone to anger an individual is, and how efficiently he or she can handle it.

However, the chances are good that if a person does have a problem in controlling anger, he or she is aware of it. People who tend to act out in ways that seem frightening or out of control often need help finding healthy ways of dealing with their emotions.

Most psychologists who specialize in anger management believe that some individuals are more prone to anger than others are. They are more hotheaded and get angry more intensely and easily than the average person does.

There are also certain types of individuals who do not exhibit anger in spectacular ways but are perpetually grumpy and irritable.

People who get angry easily do not always throw stuff, shout, and a curse. Sometimes, they sulk, withdraw into themselves, or fall physically ill.

Easily angered individuals have a low tolerance for frustration, according to psychologists, which means that they believe they should not have to face annoyance, inconvenience, or frustration. They find it difficult to take situations in stride and are extremely frustrated when situations seem somewhat unjust.

Most people believe anger to be a negative quality because they learn that it is okay to express any other emotion apart from anger.

Consequently, they do not learn how to manage it or channel it into a more positive and constructive outcome. Family background also plays a role when it comes to managing anger.

Usually, people who are quick to anger come from families that are not skilled at emotional expression, as well as chaotic and disruptive families.

It is never healthy or helpful to let it all hang out. Some individuals may use this as an excuse to hurt others. Acting out in anger usually escalates the aggression and anger and does nothing to help the person who is angry or the person he or she is angry with to deal with the problem. It is better to find ways of managing the anger by identifying what triggered it in the first place and then coming up with strategies to keep those triggers from pushing one over the edge.

Anger management involves a wide range of strategies and skills that can help with identifying the signs and symptoms of anger and handling triggers healthily and constructively. This process requires individuals to recognize anger at an early stage and to communicate their feelings and needs while remaining in control and calm. It does not involve avoiding associated feelings or holding in the feelings of anger.

Anger management is an acquired skill, which means that anyone can master this critical skill with time, dedication, and patience, and the payoff is great. Learning to manage and control anger and to express it appropriately and healthily can help people achieve their goals, build more solid relationships, and lead more satisfying and happy lives.

Whenever anger is negatively influencing a relationship or is leading to dangerous behavior, an individual may benefit from professional help, such as joining an anger management class or seeing a mental health professional. However, there are early interventions people can try. Many people find that they can effectively deal with their anger issues without resorting to professional help.

People may also choose to use counseling to control and manage their out-of-control anger, especially if it is negatively affecting their relationships and other important aspects of their lives. Licensed mental health professionals can help them find and develop a variety of effective techniques for changing their behavior and way of thinking to manage their anger better.

However, people with anger issues need to be honest with themselves and their therapist about their problem and ask about his or her approach to anger management. The approach should not be only about putting them in touch with their feelings and expressing them; rather, it should be about their precise anger problem. According to psychologists, by using professional help, a highly angry individual can move closer to a middle-range in about two to three months, depending on the technique used and the circumstances.

People with anger management issues indeed need to learn how to be more assertive, instead of becoming aggressive. However, individuals who do not feel or express enough anger should be the most avid readers of most courses and books on improving assertiveness. These individuals are more acquiescent and passive than the average person and tend to allow others to walk all over them. This is not the typical behavior of a highly angry person. Nevertheless, these books can contain some helpful techniques to employ in frustrating situations to manage anger.

Life is full of unpredictable events, loss, pain, and frustration. No one can change that; however, people can change the way they let such factors affect them. Anger management techniques can keep highly angry individuals from making angry responses that can make them unhappy in the end.

Anger Management Skills you need to have

Failure to manage one's anger often leads to a wide variety of problems, such as yelling at one's kids, health problems, saying stuff one will later regret, sending rude texts and emails, threatening one's workmates, or physical violence. However, anger management difficulties do not always have to be that serious. Nevertheless, people might just find that they waste tons of time and mental energy venting about things or people they dislike or thinking about situations that upset them.

Having anger management skills does not mean that one never gets angry. Rather, it is about learning how to identify, deal with, and express one's anger in productive and healthy ways. Everyone can learn these skills, and there is always room for improvement. Anger can range from mild irritation to full-blown rage. When left unchecked, these feelings can lead to aggressive behavior like damaging property, yelling at someone, or physically attacking someone. They may also cause people to withdraw from society and turn their anger inward.

Angry emotions turn into a serious problem when they are felt too intensely and too often, or when an individual expresses them in inappropriate and unhealthy ways. Anger management skills are meant to help people discover and use healthy strategies to express and reduce their angry feelings. Keeping one's temper in check can be quite difficult; fortunately, using a few simple anger management tips can help one to stay in control.

Cognitive Behavioral Skills

Research consistently proves that these skills are effective for improving anger management. They involve changing how a person thinks and behaves based on the notion that people's feelings, thoughts, and behaviors are all related or connected. A person's thoughts and actions or behaviors can either increase or reduce their emotions. Therefore, if people want to shift their emotional state away from feelings of anger, they need to change what they are doing and thinking about.

Cognitive-behavioral interventions for anger management involve turning away from the behaviors and thoughts that fuel one's anger. The flame of anger will not continue to burn without this fuel, which means that it will begin to die down, and one will calm down. The best strategy is to come up with a workable Anger Management and Control Plan, which will enable one to determine what to do when one starts losing cool.

Some of the most effective anger management tips include:

1.Identify the Triggers

People who have fallen into the habit of losing their cool should find it helpful to consider the things that trigger their anger, for example, fatigue, traffic jams, snarky comments, long queues, a stressful job, or other things that tend to shorten their fuse. This is not to say that they should start blaming other people or situations for their inability to keep their temper. Instead, understanding these triggers can help them plan accordingly.

They might choose to plan their day in a different way to help them manage their stress levels better. They might also employ some anger management strategies whenever they are about to encounter situations that they usually find frustrating to lengthen their fuse, which will minimize the risk of a single distressing situation, setting them off.

2.Determine Whether one's Anger is Productive or Disruptive

Before reacting to a stressful situation, people need to try to calm themselves down and ask themselves whether their anger is productive or disruptive. For example, if an individual is witnessing the violation of another person's rights, his or her anger might help find the courage to challenge the situation and changing it.

On the other hand, if a person's anger is threatening to force someone to lash out or is causing some form of distress, it may be disruptive. Therefore, it makes sense to find effective ways of changing an individual's emotions by staying calm.

3.Identify the Warning Signs

It often seems like anger overwhelms people in the blink of an eye. However, this is not the case, as there are always warning signs when one's anger is beginning to rise. It is important to recognize these signs to help one take appropriate action to rein it in and prevent it from erupting. Some of the physical warning signs of anger include clenching one's fists, increased heartbeat, or one's face feeling hot. One may also notice some cognitive changes, such as beginning to see red or feeling one's mind racing.

When people notice these warning signs, they have a good opportunity to make immediate interventions to prevent their anger from boiling over to a point where they might end up creating more and worse problems in their lives.

4.Think Before Speaking

During a heated moment, it is easy to say something stinging that one will later regret. Therefore, it is always better to take a few moments to breathe and collect one's thoughts before speaking, which will allow the other person or people involved in the situation to do likewise. Trying to stick it out or win an argument in a heated situation will only fuel one's anger. It is even better to walk away if the situation looks like it might become explosive, after explaining that one is not trying to dodge the subject. One can rejoin the discussion when one is feeling more composed.

5.Be Assertive and Express one's Anger

As soon as one is feeling calmer and thinking more clearly, one should express one's frustration in a non-confrontational but assertive manner. It is important to express one's needs and concerns directly and clearly without offending the other person or trying to control him or her.

6.Talk to a Trusted Friend

People who are experiencing feelings of anger should talk to someone who has a calming effect on them. Expressing their feelings or talking through a problem with that person may be very helpful. However, it is important to understand that venting can backfire in certain situations. For example, talking about all the reasons they dislike someone or complaining about their boss may add fuel to the flame of anger.

It is a common myth that venting makes people feel better. It can accomplish the opposite. Therefore, it is important to use this coping method with a high level of caution. A good plan of action if one is going to talk to a friend would be to work on finding a solution, not just vent. Talking with a friend about anything else other than the frustrating situation might work better.

7.Get Some Exercise

Anger tends to give people a surge of energy, which needs a productive outlet. The best way to put it to good use is to engage in exercise. Hitting the gym or going for a brisk walk will burn off the extra energy and tension. Also, engaging in regular exercise helps people decompress. Aerobic workouts, in particular, help to reduce stress, which helps improve people's tolerance levels.

8.Think in a Different Way

When people are angry, having angry thoughts tend to build up anger. Having thoughts like, "I cannot stand this traffic jam anymore," will exacerbate a person's frustration further. Therefore, when people find themselves having thoughts that fuel their anger, they should reframe them and remind themselves of the real facts, such as there are millions of vehicles on the road every day, so there are bound to be traffic jams.

Focusing on the larger picture without adding distorted facts or frustrating predictions will help people stay calmer. It might also be helpful to develop a mantra that one can repeat to drown out negative thoughts that fuel anger, for example, saying, "I am ok and things will be fine," over and over again will help keep the thoughts that fuel one's rage at bay.

9.Find Possible Solutions

Instead of focusing on the things that made them angry, people should instead work on resolving the problem at hand. For example, if a child's messy room is driving him or her parent insane, solving the problem might be as simple as closing the door. People should always remind themselves that anger rarely solves anything, and it might make the situation worse.

10.Avoid Placing Blame

A tendency to always place blame or criticize might increase tension. A good way to avoid doing this is to stick with 'I' statements when describing a frustrating situation while being specific and respectful at the same time. For example, it is better to say, "I am upset because you came late" instead of saying, "you never come on time."

11.Avoid Holding Grudges

Forgiveness is a powerful and effective tool for managing anger. When people allow negative feelings to drown out positive ones, they end up finding themselves overcome by their sense of injustice or bitterness. However, when they choose to forgive people who have angered them, they might both end up learning from their experience and strengthen their relationship.

12.Release Tension Using Humor

A little humor can diffuse tension and lighten up the dark mood. Although it is difficult to do, people who are begging to feel angry should use humor to help them face whatever is upsetting them, or even any unrealistic hopes they may have for how things should go. That said they should take care not to use sarcasm, which can make the situation worse and hurt the other person's feelings.

13.Engage in Relaxation Techniques

There are tons of relaxation techniques to choose from, and people should find a few that work best for them. Progressive muscle relaxation and breathing exercises are two of the most effective exercises for reducing tension. Better yet, someone who is feeling frustrated and angry can perform both discreetly and quickly at any time.

14.Determine the Best Time to Seek Help

Learning to manage anger is a challenge for everyone sometimes. People who think their anger has gotten out of control and is causing them to do things they never thought they could ever do should seek professional help for their problem.

15.Use a Calm Down Kit

People who tend to take out their anger on their loved ones when they come home from work stressed out should create a kit to help them calm down and relax. It can be an object that helps engage their senses, such as a portrait of a beautiful and peaceful landscape, or an inspirational or spiritual passage about staying calm.

One of the most important lessons here is that it is possible to manage anger and choose to live a life free of the negative effects of this feeling. People who struggle to manage the anger should always seek assistance; because no one should have to live life at the mercy of an emotion that should ideally lead us to fight for what is right.

Chapter 3

Types of Anger

There are lots of different combinations of anger modes. No one experiences anger quite the same as any other person. You could be someone who screams and yells at someone who makes you angry but quickly forgives and forgets as soon as they've apologized.

You could be someone who keeps your anger bottled inside but secretly hopes that the person that made you angry receives karmic justice in the form of a terrible accident.

You could be a passive-aggressive person that chooses to direct your anger at the world as a whole, being sullen and uncooperative with everyone and everything.

While the specific experience of anger may be unique to each individual, some trends result in common types of anger. These will be addressed in the following list.

Even if the way that you experience anger isn't covered in this list, you will be able to see similarities in them that you can relate to, and in recognizing these similarities, you will be one step closer to identifying the anger management strategy that will work for you.

To make this list as accessible as possible, I will propose an example scenario and each anger type will be represented by a response to this situation typical of a person who possesses that type.

The scenario is simple: you have been turned down for a promotion in favor of someone with less experience and tenure in your company.

You have worked long and hard for this promotion, only to be denied it without explanation. You are angry, perhaps rightly so.

The question is, how do you express your anger?

Assertive Anger

What Does It Look Like?

If you possess assertive anger, in response to missing out on the promotion you will stop and ask yourself why you were turned down for the promotion and how you can improve to be considered next time.

You may even go so far as to approach your boss and ask for feedback to improve. This is the most constructive type of anger expression. Feelings of frustration and anguish are used as a catalyst for positive change. Anger is confronted, analyzed objectively, and acted upon with strategy and aforethought.

If you exhibit this type of anger, you can express it without causing damage or distress to those around you.

How Do I Control It?

Assertive anger is a type of controlled anger. It is defined as being in control as long as you are using it toward positive results such as overcoming fear, addressing injustice, or achieving the desired outcome.

Chronic Anger

What Does It Look Like?

If you possess chronic anger, in response to missing out on the promotion you will become resentful toward your boss, your job, your coworkers, and even toward your friends and family.

This type of anger is ongoing and is usually internalized but quick to make an appearance if you're provoked. It is a constant feeling of frustration; frustration with yourself, those around you, or your current circumstances. It can stem from a general feeling of not being in control of your situation, which leads to feelings of hopelessness that are expressed as perpetual irritability. This type of prolonged anger can impact your health and wellbeing negatively.

How Do I Control It?

You should stop and ask yourself what the cause of your anger is.

Once the cause of your anger has been identified, you should take steps to resolve the conflict, either inside yourself or in your current situation.

This may mean finding the strength to forgive whoever you feel has wronged you or communicating your feelings clearly and constructively to the party or parties responsible so that you can come to a mutual understanding.

Whichever positive avenue you choose to deal with your anger, dealing with it will allow you to let it go and prevent it from continuing to brew inside you.

Behavioral Anger

What Does It Look Like?

If you possess behavioral anger, in response to missing out on the promotion you will feel the need to react physically.

You may respond to the news by breaking something in the office, whether it be something small like a pencil or something large like a computer. You may feel the need to scrunch up a piece of paper and aggressively throw it into the wastebasket.

However, if you demonstrate an extreme type of behavioral anger, you may act aggressively toward your boss and/or coworkers. It's even possible for you to become violent toward these people.

Behavioral anger is a type of anger that causes you to lash out physically; to express your anger with physical, typically aggressive, actions. These actions can cause physical harm to those around you, but the volatile and uncontrolled nature of your behavior can negatively impact your ability to form lasting bonds with people, as it will cause people to distrust you.

How Do I Control It?

While a physical response to anger is quite often aggressive, it's important to note that anger doesn't automatically lead to aggression or violence.

Consider some self-reflection and try to figure out why you are choosing aggression as an outlet for your anger. If you are unable to do this, try to at least identify the warning signs of your aggressive behavior.

As soon as you feel yourself exhibiting these warning signs, try to step away from the situation that is causing the anger, or manage it by telling yourself to stay calm.

Say the words out loud and couple them with some of the deep breathing and muscle relaxation techniques that we will cover further in this book. If this fails and you still feel the need to express your anger physically, take up an active but constructive hobby like working out or running.

Verbal Anger

What Does It Look Like?

If you possess verbal anger, in response to missing out on the promotion you will seek to hurt your boss with words. You may shout at them, criticize them, ridicule them, whatever you think would hurt them the most.

You will also most likely turn on your savage tongue on the coworker that was promoted ahead of you as well as anyone else that gets in the way of your tirade.

Verbal anger is similar to behavioral anger in that the anger is expressed with acts of aggression that are intended to cause harm

47

to whatever or whoever is making you angry. However, in the case of verbal anger, the harm inflicted is psychological, rather than physical.

How Do I Control It?

Breathe. Before saying anything, just breathe. The trick to controlling verbal anger is to delay your response long enough for you to prevent yourself from verbalizing your first though because that first thought is bound to be vicious.

The good thing about this type of anger is that your first reaction is verbal rather than physical, so you are already prone to expressing your anger with your words rather than your fists.

If you can stop yourself from vocalizing your first thought, you will be one step closer to being able to replace your tendency to resort to verbal abuse with a more constructive verbal expression of anger.

Judgmental Anger

What Does It Look Like?

If you possess judgmental anger, in response to missing out on the promotion you are likely to start bad-mouthing the parties involved and disparaging their worth. You might call your boss an idiot who doesn't know what they're doing.

You might say that the coworker that was promoted ahead of you is laughably unqualified for the position and that they won't last a week. You may say that the company you work for is beneath you and that you're better off working for a company that recognizes your talents.

Or you may say that the whole system is unfair and give up on any further opportunities to rise the ranks. Judgmental anger stems from a core belief that you are better than, or less than, others. It is usually the reaction of indignation to a perceived injustice or someone else's perceived shortcomings. The problem with judgmental anger is that no matter how justified your complaints maybe, they will only result in you pushing people away because you will constantly assume that the opinions of others are less valid than your own.

How Do I Control It?

The best way to manage judgmental anger is to exercise empathy and try to understand other people's viewpoints.

While you may disagree with someone's opinion, by trying to see things from their point of view, you are opening yourself up to other perspectives and potentially gaining insights that will give you more ideas on how to arrive at a positive solution.

If you can do this, you will get the bonus of people looking favorably upon you as you will have less of a tendency to come across as condescending or belittling.

Passive-Aggressive Anger

What Does It Look Like?

If you possess passive-aggressive anger, in response to missing out on the promotion you are likely to put less effort into your work going forward, procrastinating or delivering lack-luster results.

You may even become uncooperative at work, particularly when dealing with your boss or the coworker that was promoted ahead of you.

A passive-aggressive person tends to avoid expressing their anger outright and prefers to more subtle methods of venting such as non-compliance, sarcasm, or veiled mockery.

A passive-aggressive person will typically feel that this type of anger expression is less damaging than active-aggression. They may even not see their behavior as aggressive at all. However, people on the receiving end of passive-aggression usually notice the behavior change and this will cause feelings of confusion and frustration. Often, they will wish that the angry person would just confront them, rather than being passive-aggressive.

How Do I Control It?

The key to controlling passive-aggression is communication. Practice the assertive communication techniques that we will cover later in this book. Usually, passive-aggression is born from a fear of confrontation.

Try exploring this fear within yourself and little by little work on articulating your frustrations to your close friends and relatives.

Try analyzing the situation that is making you frustrated and using cognitive restructuring to come up with strategies for voicing your anger without damaging relationships.

With every successful exchange, you will see your confidence grow and your fear of confrontation melt away.

Overwhelmed Anger

What Does It Look Like?

If you possess overwhelmed anger, in response to missing out on the promotion you will not be able to control yourself.

You may break down and start crying. You may need to go somewhere private and scream your lungs out. You may need to rush to the bathroom to vomit.

Whatever form the response takes, it will be uncontrolled. Overwhelmed anger usually occurs when you feel that you don't have control over your situation or circumstances.

It is commonly experienced by people that have taken on more responsibility than they can handle or people that have been affected negatively by unexpected events. It occurs when a person feels more stress than their mind can handle.

Their mind is so full of negative thoughts that one additional trigger, even a small one, will result in a response that is strong and sudden.

How Do I Control It?

If you are experiencing overwhelmed anger you need to reach out for support. Find people to talk to, whether they are family members, friends, or coworkers.

You don't necessarily have to tell them how you're feeling, as long as you can ask them to provide you with some help and support to lighten your burden. Your life is probably so jam-packed with obligations that you can barely have time to yourself.

Balancing work, family, and a social life can be a nightmare and is bound to cause stress. By asking for help you can trim down the list of things to do, giving yourself more time and alleviating potential sources of stress.

Ask your partner to cook dinner every Wednesday night so that you can have one night a week away from the stove.

Ask your coworker to help you with your paperwork so that you take your time completing your other work.

Ask your best friend to babysit now and then so that you can have a night to yourself. Trim down your to-do list where you can and don't feel that you need to carry the entire weight of your world on your shoulders.

Self-Abusive Anger

What Does It Look Like?

If you possess self-abusive anger, in response to missing out on the promotion you will tell yourself that you didn't deserve the promotion and you were stupid to even have applied. You will swear at yourself and may even try to punish yourself with self-inflicted harm.

Self-abusive anger stems from feelings of humiliation, shame, and unworthiness. It is typically expressed internally with negative self-talk and self-harm.

Physical self-harm is particularly dangerous and can be represented in the form of self-inflicted wounds, drug use, alcoholism, or disordered eating.

Self-abusive anger has many similarities to clinical depression, though anger tends to spark action rather than inaction.

How Do I Control It?

The best way to manage self-abusive anger is to change the way you think. If your anger is self-abusive, it means you tend thoughts of self-defeat.

Exercising cognitive reframing techniques is a good way to transform these kinds of thoughts into more objective thoughts.

By learning to be objective, you will soon see that you are not always to blame, that other factors may be responsible for a situation that is causing you anguish.

Once you become better at being objective, you will be able to stop punishing yourself and think of more constructive ways to address the situation.

Retaliatory Anger

What Does It Look Like?

If you possess retaliatory anger, in response to missing out on the promotion you will become extremely defensive. You will attack your boss verbally and demand an explanation.

You will attack the coworker that was promoted ahead of you and list all the reasons why you are better suited for the position.

You may even quit your job. Retaliatory anger is an automatic and instinctive response to feelings of confrontation or aggression.

It is the need to fight back at those that have wronged you. In the case of the above scenario, you would feel that your professional abilities have been attacked and you will seek to defend these abilities while at the same time punishing those that have called them into question.

Retaliatory anger is the most common type of anger and while the resultant act of vengeance may not necessarily be deliberate, it often leads to escalation when retaliation is reciprocated in kind.

Chapter 4

Positive Thinking for Anger Free Life

We have seen how dealing with anger through avoidance is ineffective and why suppressing your anger can only lead to disaster. We explored the reasons why it is vital to manage anger with emotional intelligence and how we can cultivate it.

We are going to discuss the importance of cultivating positive thinking when dealing with anger problems.

Some of the important topics that we are going to tackle include how to change how we think, how to combat negative thoughts when they arise, and how to troubleshoot without anger.

We are also going to discuss how you can use relaxation and breathing to combat anger issues. Hopefully, you will have learned how to effectively deal with your anger in ways that are beneficial to yourself as well as the people in your life.

Change the Way You Think About Your Life

Whether you realize it or not, the way you think about yourself and your life greatly determines the quality of your life. If you constantly have happy and positive thoughts and feelings, life feels magical, exciting, and very fulfilling.

Pleasant thoughts and emotions can motivate you to take actions that improve your wellbeing and make your life more worthwhile.

You may decide to accept that job you have been hoping for or be jolted into action and open that business you've been thinking about.

On the other hand, if you are always plagued by negative thoughts, you may experience life as bleak, miserable, and dreadful.

You may find yourself withdrawn due to a fear of the world and the people in it, and you may lack the morale to make bold decisions and end up failing even at things that you are good at. Indeed, our thoughts are very reflective of our actions and can have a strong influence on the way our lives turn out to be. So, to improve the quality of our lives, we need first to change the way we think.

This, however, is easier said than done. It can be extremely difficult to be optimistic and positive when you constantly deal with anger issues.

Nevertheless, changing the way we think is fundamental if we hope to get rid of our chronic anger and begin living happily once more.

If you are wondering how you can reverse your negative thoughts and start thinking positively again, here are some of the tips which might help you overcome negative thinking.

Create Positive Affirmations

Most of us tend to make only negative affirmations as a way of dealing with our fear of disappointment. In a way, we hope that through being negative in the first place, we are preparing ourselves for scenarios where things don't work out in our favor.

If we expect to fail, we won't be too bothered when we do, right? In reality, this mindset only serves to hold us back since it diminishes our confidence in ourselves and keeps us from making bold decisions. Next time you feel like being negative, try motivating yourself with some positive self-talk instead.

Let Go of the Need be too Self-Critical

As humans, we tend towards being too hypercritical of ourselves. This is because we constantly compare ourselves with others.

We may feel like others are more advantaged than we are due to some superficial reason. Maybe we think they are too intelligent, too smart, too rich, or too talented.

This, however, is not always rooted in reality. In truth, all of us have our unique personalities with their advantages and setbacks. It is, therefore, very counterproductive for you to dwell on your deficiencies. If anything, you should use them as a motivation to grow and become better.

Appreciate Your Strengths

It is not uncommon for most people to take the things they have for granted. Many times, we complain about the things we don't have without appreciating what we do have.

For instance, instead of grumbling about the job that you failed to get, why don't you take the time to appreciate the fact that you are healthy enough to find another job? You'll be surprised at how this changes your outlook on life.

Don't Take Yourself Too Seriously

Many times, we find ourselves getting frustrated and anxious simply because we take ourselves too seriously.

We obsess over things because we think of life as some kind of competition which we have to win. This makes us anxious since we are afraid of failure.

By realizing that life is simply meant for living, we can relax and begin to enjoy ourselves instead of continually aggravating ourselves with worries and anxieties.

Like the great philosopher Alan Watts once said, "Man suffers because he takes too seriously that which the gods made for fun."

Strive to Live in the Present Moment

One of the reasons why many people struggle with anxiety and anger problems is because they simply worry too much about the past and the future.

We often tend to think that we will only be happy someday in the future when everything finally comes together in some ideal way.

The truth is that in doing so, we only postpone our happiness even as the clock of our mortality continues to tick.

It is far more beneficial and fulfilling to seek happiness in the present moment.

Take Care of Your Body

A healthy body is essential to creating happy thoughts. If your body is in distress, then you are more likely to become privy to negative self-talk and mental chatter. Ù

It is, therefore, essential to pay attention to your body's needs if you hope to improve the quality of your thoughts. The best part is that taking care of your body is not strenuous.

You simply have to practice eating healthily, engage in fitness exercises, and ensure you get enough sleep. Remember also to drink a lot of water and avoid drugs and alcohol.

When your body is adequately cared for and maintained, positive thinking naturally follows.

Focus on Yourself

It is very easy for us to see negativity and evil in other people and perceive ourselves as morally righteous. However, we all know that nobody is perfect, and everyone could use some self-improving.

So instead of constantly obsessing over the deficiencies of other people, you could turn the criticism inwards and focus on bettering those aspects of yourself, which you feel are deficient.

Have Faith in Yourself and Your Abilities

It is easy for us to lose confidence in ourselves when faced with the challenges of life. However, a lack of faith in ourselves can lead to feelings of inadequacy and victimhood, which leave us feeling powerless and resentful.

We need to cultivate self-confidence, even when we feel overwhelmed by life since this will provide us with the resilience to overcome any challenges that may beset us.

Think Differently and More Effectively When You Get Angry

Granted, feelings of anger and frustration can be very strong that they overwhelm us; it is essential to maintain a positive mindset when provoked.

Positive thinking can help us remove ourselves from the situation and evaluate it from a more objective point of view. As a result, we can be better placed to make rational choices and prevent our emotions from getting the better part of us.

Keeping a positive mindset when riled up, however, is not a very simple thing to do. The temptation to overreact can be too strong to resist when we feel seriously aggrieved by others.

Nevertheless, maintaining a positive mindset can help us deal more appropriately with our feelings of frustration without causing harm to ourselves and other people.

While you may be justifiably angry at someone for something they may have done, you need to try and keep your thinking unclouded, since this will help you make better decisions.

Here are some of the tips which can help you think differently and more effectively when you get angry:

Identify the Cause of Your Anger

Many times, we end up erupting in aggression when angry simply because we do not understand the real cause of the anger.

Frustration without apparent reason typically leads to more frustration, which can easily lead to explosive altercations when the final straw breaks. To change how you think about your anger, therefore, you need to narrow down on the real cause as soon as you feel the symptoms in your body.

This will not only prevent you from overreacting, but it will also stop you from making wrong judgments like blaming someone unfairly.

Take Yourself out of the Situation

It is very difficult to think clearly when you are smack in the middle of a situation, which triggered your anger in the first place.

To be able to resolve the problem, you need to remove yourself from your situation so that you can collect your thoughts and gain clarity. You may want to take a walk or go into your room for a few minutes.

Alternatively, read your favorite book or take your pet for a walk until you feel calm. Once the tension dissipates, you will be thinking much more clearly and thus be more capable of dealing with the problem.

Realize that you are Choosing your Response

Often, when people get provoked and react in violent ways, which gets them in trouble, they like to plead defense by saying their anger made them do it.

However, while anger can make you feel very strong emotions, ultimately, the choice on how to respond rests firmly with you.

So, before you make any rash decisions out of anger, which you may later end up regretting, you need to remind yourself that you are the one choosing how to respond. By taking responsibility for your anger in this way, you can start thinking more effectively and seek out healthy solutions for dealing with your rage.

Remember that Your Beliefs do not Necessarily Reflect Reality

It is very common for people to shift the responsibility of their anger on others instead of taking it upon themselves.

Whenever we get angry, we tend to always see others as toxic and ourselves as saintly, which only works out against us in the end.

The truth of the matter, however, is that we, ourselves, can be very toxic to ourselves as well as to other people. We may be disposing ourselves to anger by imposing our worldview and values onto others or expecting them to meet our unrealistic expectations. It is, therefore, important to remind yourself that your beliefs about what or who made you angry may not be grounded in reality.

Subjecting yourself to this criticism when angry can help you attain a realistic perspective on your anger.

Respond Instead of Reacting

It can be very difficult to maintain a cool demeanor and engage in mature discourse when fired up with rage.

Most times, when we engage in a discussion when we are angry, we are seeking validation for our hurt feelings.

We may, therefore, be more inclined to interrupt the other person, yell at them, or completely dismiss everything they say. However, this is not in any way helpful when it comes to dealing with anger.

To think more clearly and effectively about our anger, we need to listen to the other person intently and respond tactfully with clear and concise sentences. This can help us begin thinking effectively when dealing with our feelings of frustration.

Troubleshooting Without Anger

Throughout this book, we have reiterated the primacy of anger as a human emotion, as well as the role it plays in our lives.

We found out that anger can help us tackle problems of injustice that threaten the very fabric of our society. So then, dear, you probably agree that anger has a special role to play in our lives.

Nevertheless, unrestrained anger can be detrimental to the achievement of our objectives and aims.

Whether it's in our relationships with our loved ones or our professional careers, unmanaged anger can hinder progress and success.

For this reason, we must find a way of solving problems that make us angry without letting our feelings control us.

While anger can motivate us to tackle the problems we face and make our situations better, chronic anger serves no purpose other than drain useful energy, which could be channeled to more productive activities.

It is, therefore, important that our anger is managed in healthy ways and expressed in creative endeavors. Instead of using anger to destroy and tear-down ourselves and each other, we should strive to use it for the benefit of ourselves and others.

Chapter 5

How is anger treated?

There are several techniques with which it is possible to manage anger, let's see them in detail.

Visualization

This technique involves your imagination. You have to visualize yourself keeping calm amidst the anger of another person.

See yourself calm and collected, while the other person is throwing invectives at you. Picture yourself remaining calm despite the embarrassment caused by a colleague.

If you have certain events or incidents in the past that made you angry, imagine those incidents and visualize yourself acting calmly in such situations.

Your visualization must be vivid; include your facial expressions and every detail of the behavior that you would want to do.

Reflexology/Acupressure

Massaging or pressing certain trigger spots in your body can relieve pain, decrease anxiety/depression and ease anger. In the case of anger, the middle finger is involved.

All you have to do is to massage or press the length of the middle finger of your right hand for 3 to 5 minutes. Switch to your left hand and do the same. While doing these, inhale and exhale deeply.

Continue the action until your anger has subsided.

Progressive Muscle Relaxation

Again, this technique helps manage anger by relieving stress and tension in the body. It also works if you have a nagging pain or ache whenever you feel stressed.

Muscle tension is a response the body gives whenever you are stressed and tense. This could result in feelings of anger. So, progressive muscle relaxation helps relieve muscle tension to prevent anger.

You may start with the use of an audio recording to aid your memorization of the muscle groups. Once you know the muscle groups, you can do everything on your own. The best thing

Mindfulness Meditation

Mindfulness meditation is a kind of meditation that has been proven by several studies to be of immense benefit to the mind and the body.

It is a kind of mental training that teaches you self-awareness by focusing your mind on your experiences, emotions, thoughts, and sensations in the present.

Mindfulness practice may combine breathing exercises with visualization, imagery, and muscle relaxation.

This particular meditation helps very much with anger management because it trains you to become aware of your emotions, including anger before they jump on you.

It also teaches you to focus on the present without giving any thought to the past or the future and also to accept everything without judgment.

To engage in mindfulness meditation, here are the steps you can follow

Get a quiet, comfortable, and noiseless place for practice. You can either use a chair or sit on the floor. Wherever you decide to sit, ensure you sit in an upright position with your back straight but not stiff.

Clear your mind of all thoughts of the past or future while immersing yourself completely in the present. Stay grounded in the present. Draw your awareness to the rise and fall of your breath, observing the sensation that the air moving in and out produces in your body as you breathe.

Focus on the rise and fall of your belly and the in and out of the air in your nostrils and the mouth. Pay mind to the change in rhythm as you inhale and exhale.

Become aware of your thoughts as they come and go. Do not judge whatever it thought is, be it fear, worry, frustration, anxiety, or anything. Just observe as the thoughts float around in your mind.

Note that you shouldn't try to suppress the thoughts or ignore them. Simply make a mental note of them while focusing on your breathing.

If you notice yourself getting carried away in the thoughts, don't judge yourself. Simply return your mind to your breathing after taking note of the thoughts. Don't be harsh with yourself.

Once you are nearing the end of your meditation session, stay seated for one or two minutes and gradually become aware of your immediate environment. Appreciate the surrounding for a while and then slowly get up. Go about your day with your mind at rest.

In practicing mindfulness meditation, you can also incorporate it into other activities like doing the dishes, driving, exercising, or even brushing your teeth. Mindfulness is best practiced right before you go to sleep or when you just wake up.

Sound therapy

Natural sounds can be calming and therapeutic. All you have to do is to listen to the sounds of nature and they would appease you.

Lie or sit down comfortably in a place where you won't be disturbed. Listen to the sounds of the falling rain, the blowing wind, the wooing sound of the waves, the chirping of birds, the waterfalls, and similar sounds of nature. Some people prefer soft music of their favorite songs. It doesn't matter what sound you choose, provided that it calms you.

Hypnosis

Hypnosis by a certified expert can help you manage your anger, anxiety, and stress. Nevertheless, this is not recommended for persons, who have psychiatric problems. It may aggravate their condition. Also, ensure that the person performing the procedure is licensed and legitimate.

Autosuggestion

In this method, you repeatedly suggest to yourself the positive behaviors that you want to acquire. It's like hypnotizing yourself until the thoughts penetrate your subconscious and consequently, change the way you behave. This should be done at least daily. You can do it several times a day as well.

Psychologist/Psychiatrist

This is your last alternative when nothing could work for you. You need the help of a licensed expert, who will guide you in managing your anger, stress, and anxiety. Your psychologist will assist you in recognizing positive behaviors, and the advantage of choosing them over the negatives.

Chapter 6

Understanding Mental Health and Anger

Even though no succinct definition exists, mental health is essentially your frame of mind and way to deal with life. Mental, environmental, hereditary, or physiological variables profoundly affected by and large mental advancement.

What is mental illness? Mental illness weakens your capacity to perform routine assignments, cultivate healthy connections, or adapt to anger or stress. It might range from outrageous emotional episodes, silly or destructive ideas, and social problems.

How important is mental health? Your mental health hugely affects each part of your life.

Education

Persons with mental problems socially seclude themselves and create anxiety issues and fixation problems. Great mental health guarantees an inside and out instructive experience that improves social and scholarly abilities that lead to self-assurance and better evaluations.

Relationships

Mental health to a great extent adds to the working of human connections. Mental illness can hamper even fundamental connections with family, companions, and associates.

Many people experiencing mental illness think that it's difficult to support connections, have problems with responsibility or closeness, and much of the time, experience sexual health issues.

Sleep

Powerlessness to deal with stress or anxiety can cause a sleeping disorder. Regardless of whether you manage to nod off, you may awaken twelve times during the night with considerations of what turned out badly the previous day or how awful tomorrow will be. You may create serious sleeping issues that leave you depleted and less productive.

Physical health

Your mental state straightforwardly influences your body. For instance, stress can lead to hypertension or stomach ulcers. Mentally healthy people are at a lower hazard for some health issues.

Anger and Mental Health

Anger is most closely connected with anxiety. People who have anger management problems are frequently profoundly on edge and stressed.

They are regularly exceptionally working people who expect a lot from themselves and a lot from those whom they encircle themselves with.

Anger management problems are a characteristic side-effect of their life. A lot of these people have exceptionally significant levels of either generalized anxiety or social anxiety.

These two sorts of anxiety are adding to their anger management problems. It's a lot simpler for these people, typically men, to state that, "I have anger management problems," than to state that, "I experience the ill effects of social or generalized anxiety."

People with social anxiety think that it's difficult to be out in the open spots, for instance, malls, where there will be a lot of others around and where a simple exit isn't constantly present.

For instance, in a train when riding between home and work, when the train is moving, they are not ready to leave the train until the following stop. People with generalized anxiety have low strength in stressful situations in their life.

Some portion of their on-edge response to these situations is to become angry. Another mental condition related to anger is depression. A few specialists accept that depression will influence 1 out of 5 people, at any one point in time. 80% of people will endure depression at one point in their life.

So, it is an extremely, normal mental health condition. Depression can be a very baffling condition to have because there is no obvious solution to it. This is particularly disappointing for goal-driven people who frequently experience the ill effects of anger problems in any case.

There's no solution to it. No obvious solution to it. They can't go for a run or drink some lager, drink some alcohol, or eat some nourishment or converse with somebody about it.

Depression is a lot more perplexing than that. A typical response to depression and anger is to take the disappointment out on others. Once more, it's important that people see the truth about depression, and get it evaluated and treated.

Anger Management Is an Inability to Handle Negative Emotions

Recollect your life now. What do you do at whatever point you have a negative emotion? For instance, when you are down or on edge or stressed what do you do?

Do you sit alone unobtrusively and deal with it time permitting? Or then again do you attempt to dispose of it through alcohol, work out, Facebook, Twitter, Twitter, drugs, smoking, conversing with companions or family?

The vast majority will do the last mentioned because we've never been instructed how to deal with our negative emotions.

Lamentably for a great many people, our emotions resemble an exciting ride. It goes up when we have strong, positive emotions. It levels when we have unbiased emotions. It plunges when we have negative emotions for a specific timeframe, and afterward the cycle proceeds.

Tips on How to Improve Your Emotional and Mental Health

Your present lifestyle may not be advantageous in keeping up your emotional and mental health. Our general public is overworked, overstressed, and excessively centered around things that don't bolster great psychological prosperity.

Being proactive and doing things that cultivate great mental health can be a ground-breaking approach to enhance the nature of your day-to-day life.

Apply these tips regularly: Cooperate with others. Having positive and healthy associations with others has an important impact on psychological health. Cooperating and associating with others will prevent you from feeling forlorn.

If you disconnect yourself, don't get out of the house other than work, and run tasks, you rapidly can turn out to be desolate and start feeling discouraged. Rather find something to do that gets you out of the house and around people.

Keep your body healthy. Poor physical health can result in difficulties with mental health. The better you feel physically, the better you'll feel psychological, as well.

Make it a propensity for consistently practicing and it doesn't need to be in a rec center, you can take a run or walk your dog.

Swimming is additionally a decent exercise technique. Whatever it is that gets your body going and gets your pulse up. Practicing discharges endorphins and endorphins make you feel great, loose, and calm.

Build up a goal and endeavor to meet it. There will most certainly be some stress and challenges along the way, yet it will be well justified, despite all the trouble once you achieved those. Learn how to deal with stress viably. A large portion of us makes them calm propensities that may appear to be viable yet as a general rule neglect to address the reason for stress. A few of us deal with stress in ways that make the situation more awful.

In case you're monetarily stressed, eating a tub of frozen yogurt will at present leave you broke, yet you'll likewise wind up putting on weight. Look for positive solutions.

Exercises, for example, working out, investing energy with a friend, or perusing a book can be healthy alternatives for bringing down your stress.

Make time for yourself where you can loosen up and unwind.

Stressing over something you have no control over isn't healthy and doesn't help in settling the problem or issue. Ù

For instance, if you have cash issues and your stress and stress over it, it won't take care of the problem, it's just a motivation for you to stress out considerably more.

Rather take a full breath and think of an arrangement to diminish your costs in specific zones to have cash for progressively important things.

Invest energy every day on an agreeable action. It could be taking your dog for a walk, going for a run, going out to see a movie, get a back rub, or in any event, playing with your children.

It doesn't matter what it is you do, as long as you appreciate doing it and focus on things other than work or things you have to complete or take care of. Make space for a bit of "personal time."

Practice the specialty of forgiveness. Anger and hard feelings achieve close to nothing. They put you in a horrendous mental cycle that corrupts your sense of prosperity.

Consistently you're angry or upset the second you're troubled. Accept things as lessons learned and proceed onward as opposed to harping on the things that occurred before. Give your time to other people. Helping somebody in need is a great method to support how you feel about yourself. It's additionally a great method to meet others that are likewise thoughtful and giving.

Consider a gathering of people you'd prefer to help and find an association that helps them. It could likewise be a friend, coworker, or somebody you just met, if they are in urgent need, give them a hand, and regardless of whether it's simply discussing with them, some simply need somebody that tunes in and cares.

Learn how to quiet your mind. Your mind seldom gets a rest, not even while you're sleeping. Throughout the night, you're likely hurling, turning, and dreaming.

There are numerous ways to rest your mind: asking, contemplating, and rehearsing mindfulness are only a couple.

Our brains are restless. They're continually thinking, foreseeing, and recalling. Regardless of whether you don't see that you are contemplating something, your subliminal mind thinks constantly.

Learn how to control yours. Meditation can assist you with learning how to quiet down your mind. It might take a couple of attempts because our minds continue straying and don't have any desire to be quiet; however, with practice, you'll arrive.

Request help. If you break your arm, you look for medicinal help. In case you're having a psycho-intelligent issue, there's no explanation not to do likewise.

Regardless of what your challenge might be, there's somebody accessible with the skill to help.

You don't need to see an advocate or advisor if you don't have any desire to; you could essentially go to your family or friends, even a minister or anybody eager to tune in and to give you some assistance. Sometimes we can't do everything all alone. Requesting help isn't a shortcoming, rather, it shows quality since you recognize that you can't do it all alone and you demonstrate solidarity to connect with somebody who can support you.

Keep a journal. Writing down your considerations on paper following a long, hard day is restorative. It discharges pressure and can give you an alternate point of view.

When writing in a journal, you can be as obtuse and legit as you need without stressing over upsetting anybody with what you state since it is for your eyes as it were. It resembles a punching pack, on terrible days you can let out the entirety of your anger and dissatisfaction, and on great days you can share your fervor and fun things which will be great recollections and great jolts of energy when you have an awful day.

Emotional and mental health are both basic to your general prosperity. At the point when any segment of your health is enduring, it turns out to be substantially more testing to be a viable parent, life partner, friend, or representative.

All parts of your life, particularly your physical health, can endure. Utilize these tips to address your psychological health. In case you're not feeling better, it's time to look for help.

Chapter 7

Understanding & Handling Anger in Relationships

In this chapter, you'll discover how anger follows a predictable cycle in romantic relationships, and how you can keep it from driving you and your partner apart.

You'll learn some key communication skills that will empower you both. Most of the techniques and ideas in this section also apply to handling problems in family relationships and friendships.

The Cycle of Anger in Relationships

Angry people often have angry relationships. Usually, one person feels mistreated or frustrated, which kick starts a destructive cycle that drags both partners down.

The cycle normally goes like this:

- Partner A becomes angry because they believe that Partner B has treated them badly.

This mistreatment—which can be actual or perceived—could be trivial or major. For example, Partner A might believe that Partner B has been flirting with someone at work and feel angry as a result.

- Partner A engages in negative, destructive behaviors.

Because Partner A doesn't know how to handle their own emotions or start a calm conversation with their partner, they resort to destructive behavior instead. They may use overt forms of aggression, such as shouting or passive-aggressive tactics like sulking.

- Partner B notices Partner A's behaviors.

Unless they are willfully oblivious, Partner B will pick up on Partner A's anger. Partner B will feel attacked, blamed, and possibly rejected.

- Partner B becomes angry at Partner A.

If they don't have the skills to start a constructive dialogue with Partner A, Partner B responds with their anger.

The cycle continues. Over time, both partners may slip into a state of habitual anger. The underlying issues are never resolved. One or both partners might lash out, but neither knows how to reach a mutual understanding.

If this cycle continues long enough, both people can become resentful of one another. They may start believing that their relationship is doomed. They stop enjoying one another's company and may split up.

Sometimes this is the best solution; not all relationships are destined to work out. However, many relationships could be saved if both partners take the time to master basic communication skills and simple anger management techniques.

Exercise: The Anger Cycle in Your Relationship

Think back to the last time you felt angry at your partner. How did both of you move through the anger cycle? What happened to make you or your partner so angry? Did you manage to resolve the issue, or is it still causing problems in your relationship?

How to Shut the Cycle Down Before It Begins

The good news is that the cycle isn't inevitable. If you learn how to communicate your wants and needs in a relationship and address problems as they arise, you can enjoy a more harmonious life together.

Try these strategies:

1. Reframe your partner's behavior

Suppose your partner promised to cook dinner one evening. You come home from work and find your partner watching TV instead, with no sign that they are even thinking about making a meal. How would you respond? You could berate them for being lazy. Or you could take a passive-aggressive approach, perhaps by ignoring them and sighing as you start making your dinner. Both responses would let them know you are disappointed and angry.

Alternatively, you could try a different tactic and reframe the situation. You could ask, "What would be a more charitable interpretation of their behavior here?" In this instance, you might say to yourself, "There's no evidence that they've forgotten completely. They might have lost track of the time, or maybe they were waiting until I got home so we could talk for a while before they start cooking."

How do you think you'd speak and act towards your partner if you chose to reframe their behavior like this? You'd probably be more patient, ask straightforward questions instead of berating them, and focus on the facts rather than starting a fight.

[Of course, some behaviors can't and shouldn't be reframed. If your partner is behaving in an abusive way, it's not helpful or safe to reframe their actions. Focus on keeping yourself safe instead.]

2. Distance yourself from the situation

In the last chapter, you learned about self-distancing. Take a step back and imagine that one of your friends or relatives were in your situation.

Watch the scenario play out as though it were happening to someone else instead. What would you advise them to do?

3. Use constructive communication to resolve your differences instead of just expressing anger

This is the most important step. The best way to break the anger cycle is to start a mature, mutually beneficial conversation with your partner. Respectful conversations:

- Give all parties the chance to make their views known
- Are honest
- Come from a place of mutual compassion
- Are never abusive
- Can be difficult and draining, but allow both sides to work towards a solution

Here are a few things to keep in mind:

1. Using insults and generalizations only makes things worse

Insulting someone puts them on the defensive. If your partner insults you, don't pay them back in kind. It's better to walk away completely than let yourself be drawn into a mud-slinging match.

2. Shouting is never helpful

Shouting can feel cathartic, but it escalates the conflict. It invites hostility and keeps your body in a state of high alert. Your partner will probably shout back, and both of you will feel worse.

3. Seeking to understand, rather than persuade, is the best tactic

Are you more concerned with winning, or do you want to reach an understanding? If you treat every conversation like a battleground, your partner will soon realize that you don't want to work with them - you only want to be right.

Put your ego to one side and concentrate on gathering information. Don't minimize your partner's feelings by telling them to "calm down," and don't imply they are overreacting.

4. Planning for difficult conversations is a smart idea

It's OK to plan a conversation. It might seem strange, but writing down the points you want to cover and even rehearsing how you will explain your point of view can be very helpful.

Exercise: Planning for a Sensitive Conversation

Are there any ongoing problems in your relationship? If you and your partner keep arguing about the same "hot button" topic over and over again, it's time to try a new approach. Instead of waiting for the subject to come up in conversation and then repeating your usual points, make some notes on how the issue makes you feel, what you'd like you and your partner to do differently, and a few ideas on how the two of you could work together to come up with solutions to your problems.

Ask your partner when the two of you can discuss the issue. Using notes will help you structure the conversation and prevent you from getting overwhelmed.

5. Giving each other time to talk, checking your understanding, then swapping roles lets you both feel heard

Decide who will speak first. Flip a coin if you can't decide. Set a timer for 3-5 minutes. The first speaker gets to talk, uninterrupted, while the timer is running.

The listener's job is to do whatever it takes to keep themself from butting in while trying to understand what their partner is saying.

When the speaker has finished, the listener paraphrases the main points to check that they've understood what was said. The partners then swap roles.

Only after each person has had a chance to express their views do they work together to solve their problems. Trying to jump straight to the problem-solving stage won't work.

If you interrupt your partner when it's their turn to talk, apologize immediately and ask them to keep going. If your partner interrupts you when it's your turn to speak, pause the timer, calmly wait until they have finished, then say, "I'm going to talk again now.

Please don't interrupt until the time is up." If they can't respect this boundary, take a time out and resume the conversation later.

6. Use "I" statements when talking about your feelings

"I" statements are less confrontational than sentences that begin with "You," which often come across as aggressive or judgmental. Avoid starting sentences with "You always," "You never," or "You should."

Instead, begin with a statement about the other person's behavior, then follow up by explaining how it makes you feel.

For example, instead of saying, "You never do your share of the housework!" it would be more constructive to say, "When you leave your dirty dishes in the sink every day for me to clean, I feel unappreciated."

Next, spell out what you want from the other person. Keep your requests reasonable and specific. To continue with the example above, you could say, "I would like you to clean up every other day because this means we are splitting the job equally."

7. Notice patterns

Good communication depends on both parties being willing to put in the necessary effort. If your partner doesn't want to cooperate, don't drive yourself crazy by holding onto the hope that their communication skills will improve.

In some cases, you might even need to think about whether you want to continue with the relationship.

For example, if you've been trying all the techniques in this chapter for several weeks, yet your partner seems uninterested in understanding your feelings or making positive changes, you need to realize that your wellbeing just isn't as important to them as theirs is to you.

8. Don't make unfounded accusations

Before accusing your partner of doing something wrong, stop for a moment and ask yourself whether your suspicions are supported by evidence. A gut feeling or hunch doesn't count.

9. Don't drag up the past

Unless it's directly relevant to whatever problems you're having in the present, leave the past where it belongs.

Many couples get drawn into discussions and arguments about people and events that have no bearing on their current problems, which only makes it harder to tackle issues that affect them in the present.

10. Don't use sarcasm

Sarcasm is a form of mockery, and mockery has no place in respectful conversations. It achieves nothing, aside from aggravating your partner. If you catch yourself making a sarcastic remark, apologize immediately.

11. Watch your body language

Check that your words, tone of voice, and body language are in alignment. Keep your tone of voice steady, keep your arms and legs uncrossed, and avoid staring or using another hostile body language.

12. Don't stonewall

Psychologist and relationship expert John Gottman has identified four signs that a relationship is in trouble: criticism, contempt, defensiveness, and stonewalling.

To stonewall, someone means to withdraw or shut down when they are trying to talk to you, and it isn't a healthy response to conflict. Calling a timeout is a good idea if an argument is spiraling out of control or you aren't making any progress, but don't withdraw completely.

Chapter 8

Triumph Over Anger and Depression

Anger usually occurs as a natural response to feeling attacked, frustrated, or even being humiliated. It is human nature to get angry.

The fury, therefore, is not a bad feeling per se, because, at times, it can prove to be very useful. How is this even possible?

Anger can open one's mind and help them identify their problems, which could drive one to get motivated to make a change, which could help in molding their lives.

When is Anger a Problem?

Anger, as we have just seen, is normal in life. The problem only comes in when one cannot manage their anger, and it causes harm to people around them or even themselves.

How does one notice when their anger is becoming harmful? When one starts expressing anger through unhelpful or destructive behavior, or even when one's mental and physical health starts deteriorating. That's when one knows that the situation is getting out of hand.

It is the way a person behaves that determines whether or not they have problems with their anger. If the way they act affects their life or relationships, then there is a problem, and they should think about getting some support or treatment.

What is Unhelpful Angry Behavior?

Anger may be familiar to everyone, but people usually express their rage in entirely different ways. How one behaves when they are angry depends on how much control they have over their feelings.

People who have less control over their emotions tend to have some unhelpful angry behaviors.

These are behaviors that cause damage to themselves or even damage to people or things around them.

They include:

- **Inward Aggression.** This is where one directs their anger towards themselves. Some of the behaviors here may include telling oneself that they hate themselves, denying themselves, or even cutting themselves off the world.
- **Non-Violent or Passive Aggression.** In this case, one does not direct their anger anywhere; rather, they stick with the feeling in them. Some of the behaviors here may include ignoring people, refusing to speak to people, refusing to do tasks, or even deliberately doing chores poorly or late. These types of behaviors are usually the worst ways to approach such situations. They may seem less destructive and harmful, but they do not relieve one of the heavy burdens that are causing them to be angry.

Weigh Your Options

In life, many things may be out of one's control. These things vary from the weather, the past, other people, intrusive thoughts, physical sensations, and one's own emotions.

Despite all these, the power to choose is always disposable to any human. Even though one might not be able to control the weather, one can decide whether or not to wear heavy clothing. One can also choose how to respond to other people.

The first step, therefore, in dealing with anger is to recognize a choice.

Steps to Take in Managing Anger

A "Should" Rule is Broken. Everybody has some rules and expectations for one's behavior, and also for other people's behavior. Some of these rules include, "I should be able to do this," "She should not treat me like this," and, "They should stay out of my way." Unfortunately, no one has control over someone else's actions.

Therefore, these rules are always bound to be broken, and people may get in one's way. This can result in anger, guilt, and pressure.

It is, therefore, essential to first break these "should" rules to fight this anger. The first step to make in breaking these rules is to accept the reality of life that someone usually has very little control over other people's lives.

The next step is for one to choose a direction based on one's values. How does one know their values? One can identify their values by what angers them, frustrates them, or even enrages them.

For example, let's take the rule of "They should stay out of my way." This rule may mean the values of communication, progress, or even cooperation. What do these values mean to someone? Does one have control over them?

Finally, one can act by their values. To help with this, here are two questions one should ask themselves:

- What does one want in the long run?
- What constructive steps can one take in that direction?
- What Hurts?

The second step is to find the real cause of pain or fear after breaking the rules. These rules usually do not mean the same as one's body. This is because some states of being can hurt one's self-esteem more than others.

To understand this better, let's take the example of Susan, who expects that no one should talk ill of her. Then suddenly John comes up to her and says all manner of things to her. This, therefore, makes Susan enraged. In such a scenario, Susan should ask herself what hurts her. The answer to this question will bring out a general belief about John and herself.

She will think that "John is rude," "She is powerless," or even that "She is being made the victim." All these thoughts may hurt her.

What may even hurt her most is that she has no control over John's behavior.

Once she has noted that she has no control, she may now consider seeing John's words as a mere opinion rather than an insult. This will make her not see herself as a victim, but as a person just receiving a piece of someone else's mind about herself.

Hot Thoughts

After one has identified what hurts them, it is now time to identify and, most importantly, replace the hot, anger-driven, and reactive thoughts with more level-headed, more relaxed, and reflective thoughts. Here are some fresh ideas that may be of importance to someone:

- Hot thought: "How mean can he be!"
- A cool thought: "He thinks he is so caring."
- Hot thought: "They are stupid!"
- A cool thought: "They are just human."

Anger

All the above steps, as one may have noticed, relate to the thoughts. This is because one has first to tackle the ideas before now getting to the emotion.

In this step, therefore, one is going to respond to the anger arousal itself. There are three ways that one can follow to respond to this emotion:

One may indulge in relaxation. This relaxation can come in many forms, like enjoying some music, practicing some progressive muscle relaxation like yoga, and also visualization.

One may also use that feeling to do some constructive work. When one is angry, there is usually a large amount of energy that one uses at that time.

This is the reason that when angry, one can break down things that they would never break when calm. Imagine, therefore, how much that energy would do for someone if just directed to some constructive work.

One may also try to redefine anger when one gets angry. What does this mean? Once a person is angry, one can try to remind themselves of how anger is a problem that fuels aggression and can cause harm to loved ones and even oneself.

Moral Disengagement

In simple words, this step will help one examine the beliefs that turn anger into aggression. These beliefs usually act as mere excuses or justification for destructive acts.

Some of these beliefs include "I don't care," "This is the only way I can get my point across," or even "It is high time they recognize me." These beliefs need to be identified early enough and gotten rid of before they can con one into throwing one's morals aside.

One sure way of getting rid of them is by reminding oneself of the cost of such beliefs and the advantages of striving for understanding.

Aggression

In this step, one now needs to examine the behaviors that arise from aggression and try to fight them. Fighting these behaviors can be achieved if one calms down and puts themselves in the other person's shoes. This will help one understand why the other person is acting in such a manner, what they may be feeling, or even what they may be thinking. This approach will help to decrease the anger for all parties involved.

Increase the chance of having a reasonable conversation with the parties involved, and thus everybody is heard.

Conclusion

It is unthinkable for somebody to never get irate. Things dependably happen in our lives that make us furious and need to lash out. Nobody is impeccable and it is alright to show feeling and get upset. Be that as it may, a few individuals can't control their anger and they get way out of line.

An answer for them is to take anger management courses to remain calm and to express it more suitably and respectably.

At the point when anger is bungled, it can make many issues for the individual who is agitated as well as particularly for people around them.

Residential misuse is a colossal issue for somebody who can't control their anger. A man or lady may need to lash out at their mate on the off chance that they are furious and this makes a lot of issues in their marriage and even with their kids.

Individuals who have gone to anger management courses figure out how to channel that anger so it's not damaging.

Street wrath is another issue brought on by blundered anger. Individuals will get past irate on the off chance that somebody cuts them off.

In compelling instances of street fury, individuals have been shot or gravely harmed. Separation is a typical issue when a mate has an anger management issue.

Nobody needs to associate with a man who is constantly furious and can't remain calm. As much as a man may adore another, there is continually something that they can't endure. It can be truly hard to watch adoration blur away in face of an issue with anger.

To maintain a strategic distance from any of these circumstances, numerous individuals are thinking that it was supportive to search out proficient help. One of the best streets for this is anger management courses. It is not something to be humiliated of on the off chance that you need help remaining calm.

If you are reluctant about seeing somebody eye to eye you can simply discover help on the web. Notwithstanding anger management classes, you can likewise use things like sound tapes and books to cause figure out how to move the negative sentiments into more positive ones.

Being frantic doesn't need to result in fierce conduct or undue anxiety. One of the things that a great many people with anger issues don't understand is how their upheavals influence other individuals.

When they get some direction in how to deal with their anger, they can start to perceive how much quieter and more content everybody around them is, the point at which they aren't shouting and shouting because something didn't go an incredible way they needed.

There is no utilization in packaging antagonistic emotions any longer. It does not just harm you and the individuals around you that you think about the most, yet it likewise isn't solid.

Anger management courses will help you feel a ton better and truly begin getting a charge out of a more satisfied, all the more satisfying life.

Do you ever get irate in trivial circumstances? What circumstances are these? It is safe to say that you are ready to control your anger soon? The responses to every one of these inquiries would let you know a ton about the sort of identity you have.

Anger management assumes the main part in identity improvement. Most men and ladies think that it was exceptionally hard to manage anger and wind-up having circumstances out of extents. This additionally turns into an identity obstacle as a part of their identity improvement furthermore causes different wellbeing issues. Anger is likewise considered as one of the greatest foes of a human body and soul. It weakens judgment, can make a man rough and the individual can even lose his/her connections.

Along these lines, it is critical to figure out how to control anger or, maybe, to figure out how to channelize it in such a route, to the point that it might be useful.

Numerous advantages you can pick up from having the capacity to deal with your anger.

One may never comprehend the blissful advantages of anger management classes unless they encounter it and see an identity change as a part of their identity.

page intentionally left blank

Depression and Anxiety Therapy

Overcoming Depression and Anxiety

Howard Patel

Depression and Anxiety Therapy

Written by Howard Patel

First Edition

Copyrights Notice

Limited Liability

Please note that the content of this book is based on personal experience and various information sources.

Although the author has made every effort to present accurate, up-to-date, reliable, and complete information in this book, they make no representations or warranties concerning the accuracy or completeness of the content of this book and specifically disclaim any implied warranties of merchantability or fitness for a particular purpose.

Your particular circumstances may not be suited to the example illustrated in this book; in fact, they likely will not be. You should use the information in this book at your own risk.

All trademarks, service marks, product names, and the characteristics of any names mentioned in this book are considered the property of their respective owners and are used only for reference. No endorsement is implied when we use one of these terms.

This book is only for personal use. Please note the information contained within this document is for educational and entertainment purposes only and no warranties of any kind are declared or implied. Readers acknowledge that the author is not engaged in providing any kind of medical, dietary, nutritional, psychological, psychiatric advice, nor professional medical advice.

Please consult a doctor, before attempting any techniques outlined in this book. Nothing in this book is intended to replace common sense or medical consultation or professional advice and is meant only to inform. By reading this book, the reader agrees that under no circumstances is the author responsible for any losses, direct or indirect, which are incurred as a result of the use of the information contained within this document, including, but not limited to, errors, omissions, or inaccuracies.

Table of Contents

Introduction

Depression is a disorder — a mood disorder that affects how an individual behaves feels, thinks, reacts, interacts for a long time (continuous reoccurrence of this disorder for a minimum of two weeks shows you are depressed).

The results or symptoms of this disorder can range from fatigue and hopelessness to physical pain, loss of interest in Life, or suicidal thoughts. In the diagnostic and statistical manual (DSM-5), it was stated that when a person sees these symptoms or signs continuously within the same two weeks or more, he or she is experiencing a depressive disorder.

Depression, which tends to occur more in women than in men, is the direct result of these lingering thoughts. The way it manifests itself can vary depending on a person's age and gender.

In men, it may be seen in symptoms such as tiredness, irritability, and sometimes anger. Men tend to behave more recklessly when they are depressed, which can be seen by their abuse of drugs or alcohol.

These behaviors may often be passed off as masculine, so they are less likely to recognize it as depression and are not inclined to seek help or treatment.

Women in a depressed state are more likely to appear sad and have deep feelings of worthlessness and guilt.

They may be reluctant to take part in social activities or engage with others, even those who are close to them. Depression in children will also be different. Young children may refuse to go to school or show signs of separation anxiety when parents leave.

Teenagers are more likely to be irritable, sulky, and often get into trouble in school. In more extreme cases, you might see signs of an eating disorder or substance abuse.

Chapter 1

Signs, Symptoms, and Causes of Anxiety and Depression

Experiencing intermittent anxiety is common and a normal part of life. Nevertheless, individuals with anxiety disorders often have excessive, intense, and persistent fear and worry about everyday circumstances and events. Usually, anxiety disorders involve recurrent episodes of unexpected feelings of intense fear, terror, and nervousness that reach the peak within minutes, also known as panic attacks.

Warning Signs and Symptoms of Anxiety and Depression

You may pinpoint the cause and origin of depression if it is tied to a life event, for instance, the death of a loved one, the end of a relationship, or job loss. Sometimes we feel depressed and cannot identify a clear reason. Either way, symptoms, and signs of depression ought to be taken seriously.

The symptoms of depression may vary in different people. As mentioned earlier in this book, we have many different types of depression with some being more serious and severe than others. We will look at the symptoms of common depressions that affect a larger population.

Major depression can be devastating. Some individuals have a single major depressive episode while others may have several.

Major depression may last for two weeks or more. The main symptoms of major depression include:

- Low mood
- Suicidal thoughts or attempts
- Loss of energy
- Poor concentration
- Loss of interest in life

- Appetite and weight changes
- Hard time making decisions
- Insomnia or sleeping excessively

Major depressive disorder can also happen without an apparent reason. It may be brought on by events like:
- Death of a loved one
- Illness
- Divorce
- Other influential life changes

If one suffers from major depression, they may feel like life is no longer meaningful or worth living. It is hard to envision life being any better. That is the mental disorder talking.

[IMPORTANT] The person must seek depression treatment to get a reprieve from severe depression symptoms.

Persistent depression disorder (PDD) is less severe than major depression, but they do share some symptoms. Individuals with PDD suffer low mood for two years or longer.

PDD is at times referred to as high-functioning depression. Friends and family may not guess that one is struggling with this disorder because they seem to do fine at school or work.

One may be sad, tired, and feel bad about himself most of the time. Individuals with PDD are likely to have major depressive episodes.

Some research indicates that approximately 75 percent of people with PDD have struggled with major depression occasionally.

Seasonal affective disorder (SAD) occurs at specific times of the year. One is likely to fall into depression symptoms during winter when the days are shorter and typically end in the spring.

Most of the affected persons have mild symptoms while others experience symptoms that are likely to make them withdraw.

SAD symptoms may include:
- Low energy
- Isolation
- Sleep issues
- Carbohydrate cravings
- Overeating and weight gain

Situational depression, well-known as an adjustment disorder, stems from issues and problems with a certain situation. One can easily identify why they are depressed. Some of the issues that may lead or contribute to situational depression include:
- Divorce
- Involvement in an accident
- Death of a loved one
- Developing a serious illness
- Involvement in a crime

In some scenarios, situational depression may develop into major depression. Hence, it's advisable to speak out or see a mental health professional ensure symptoms do not worsen.

Bipolar disorder, also known as manic depression, is a mood disorder. People experiencing this depression have mood swings that revolve around extreme lows and extreme highs.

These cycles are called depressive episodes and manic episodes. The time taken between the mood shifts may vary from a few times in a year to several times in a week.

Manic episodes may feel exhilarating while bipolar depression may feel very dark. One is likely to enjoy the manic episodes but may dread the depression episodes.

This depression is a disruptive and troublesome condition that causes significant problems in an individual's life and their relationships. They should have behavioral therapy to manage the bipolar symptoms. Atypical depression is characterized by uncommon and unpredictable depression symptom patterns, and it can last for two weeks or more.

One may feel sad most of the time though certain events and circumstances may lift their mood. An individual may also feel some physical symptoms which may include:

- Fatigue
- Low mood that is lifted with some good news or positive external events
- A feeling of physical heaviness in your body
- Weight gain or appetite increase
- Extreme sensitivity to rejection
- Sleeping more but still feeling tired

Premenstrual dysphoric disorder (PMDD) may affect some women, causing them to suffer depression symptoms during their period.

Depression is more disruptive than what most people think of as PMS. The symptoms of PMDD include:

- Mood swings
- Hopelessness
- Difficulty concentrating
- Self-criticism
- Tiredness
- Severe anxiety or stress
- Food cravings and binges
- Crying spells
- Irritability
- Body aches

If you frequently struggle with some of these common symptoms of depression, you need behavioral therapy and, if necessary, may need to check in with a mental health professional for further help.

For anxiety, the symptoms are more of the same. We have listed them below. The same symptoms might still be seen in other forms of depressions not discussed above. These symptoms may include:

- Feelings of sadness, emptiness, despair, and hopelessness
- Irritability and guilt
- Loss of interest in previously enjoyable activities
- Feelings of severe tiredness and exhaustion
- Poor concentrate or memory loss
- Attempts of suicide or suicidal thoughts
- Disinterest in relationships and daily activities
- Changes in appetite
- Insomnia, sleeping too much or too little
- Feeling out of control
- Lack of energy
- Feelings of tearfulness and mood swings
- Feelings of tension
- Feeling, agitated, irritable, or angry because of trivial inconveniences or for no reason.
- Feelings of worthlessness
- Restlessness
- Pains and aches without a medical condition

Causes of Depression

Experts do not believe there is one cause of depression, but it involves several external and internal factors.

Most people possess a genetic predisposition to depression, i.e., internal. At times that could be adequate to cause intense depressive symptoms with certain circumstances.

Sometimes external factors stimulate depressive symptoms. These external factors are likely to lead to depression in individuals who do not possess any genetic predisposition.

The external factors may include:

Chronic illness

Traumatic events, e.g., rape, violence, and natural disaster, complex trauma, often resulting from childhood abuse or neglect

Conditions that can lead to shaking off the brain's balance of norepinephrine and serotonin, e.g., substance abuse, eating disorder, compulsive gambling, compulsive sexual behaviors, etc.

There is a multitude of psychological, genetic, social, and hormonal factors that come into play when referring to the causes of depression in human beings.

Biology and Hormones

Biologically speaking, it is indicated that depression runs in the blood of families with evidence that there are some genetic makeups prone to depression while some genetic makeups are more resistant to it.

Psychological Causes

When it comes to psychological causes of depression, women are more prone to them than men. Women are more likely to harbor and rehash negative feelings during bouts of depression as compared to men, who tend to be more emotional.

Social Causes

Choice of relationships, coping skills, and lifestyle decisions affect people differently. People are likely to suffer depression from a relationship or marital problems, work-life balance issues, stressful life events, and financial troubles.

Stressful events in life take part in developing and leading an individual to be depressed. Ongoing conflicts between individuals or groups affect our well-being, just like environmental and social stressors. These social stressors can be financial difficulties, unemployment, retirement, loneliness, childbirth, or the loss of something important or someone.

Invulnerable individuals, these unkind life events may be adequate to worsen a depressive disorder. An individual's personality characteristics are a significant factor.

When human beings get depressed, they habitually view themselves and the world very negatively. We tend to not appreciate the good things, and the bad things overwhelm us.

Some individuals view things in this manner even when they aren't depressed. This means they may have a depressive personality style.

The other possible cause of anxiety and depression is medications or physical illness. Hepatitis, glandular fever, alcohol and other substances of abuse, diabetes, influenza, thyroid hormones, birth control pills, anemia, and other medications like those for treating blood pressure or heart conditions may all bring about symptoms of depression.

The other conditions that have been proven to bring about depression include conditions such as strokes, HIV/AIDS, Parkinson's disease, and diabetes among others.

Recognizing the Symptoms

In this section, I will discuss how to recognize the symptoms of depression by using my anecdote.

When I went to the hospital, I found out how to detect the symptoms of depression in myself, which enabled me to offer some prescriptive advice for recognizing if a person is depressed.

The information I acquired from the therapists and psychiatrists at the hospital allowed me to come up with ways of coping with the symptoms of depression that I still use today.

Symptoms of Depression

Often, we don't realize that we are drifting into a depressive state until it is too late and then we are deep in it.

Before I became educated in mental health through the various experiences I had, I tended to fall into depression and stay there without realizing that I had gotten there in the first place.

I didn't know how to recognize the early warning signs of depression and whether I was drifting into the danger zone.

Early Warning Signs

Becoming depressed is a process and it usually starts with changes in a person's routine. If things get too out of balance in a person's daily life, things start to tip over and depression can easily get in the way.

One of the most important things that can change is sleeping.

When a person is sleeping too much or too little, things start to get strange. You start feeling too tired to do things. Your energy level tanks and then you recognize that you are starting to lose it. Sleep is one of the most important aspects of our lives because our bodies and mind need to restore themselves following a long day.

When the body does not get rest, it can easily shift into a dangerous area, where there is no energy and that can cause us to become depressed.

This was one way I recognized that my depression was beginning. When my sleep cycle started getting off, my tendency to get depressed greatly increased.

Second, when you start decreasing your time spent with people, you are starting to slip into depression. People who suffer from depression often do so in isolation and silence.

They don't want others to know they are feeling depressed, so they ghost and get out of others' lives.

This causes them to feel empty inside. But social isolation only exacerbates the problem, because the more time you spend alone, the lonelier and more depressed you feel. Moreover, this can cause a person to go off the edge and end up depressed.

Third, when a person's appetite shifts and they no longer eat well or eat too much, things also start to go awry with mood and emotions.

Because our body is either taking in too many nutrients or not enough, energy levels start to tank and cause us to feel immensely tired and unable to tackle everyday situations.

This leads to a depressed mindset that is sluggish and unable to concentrate or get things done normally.

Fourthly, whenever we start to feel immensely tired or burned out, the body starts to break down.

Physically, we are exhausted from everything and cannot function as well as we could before, so we start to lose more energy.

When this happens, we can easily enter into a phase of depression where we are no longer able to move our bodies.

We feel stuck and slowed down by the things that have caused us to feel this way. Consequently, we feel sad and down because we are not able to do the things we were able to do before.

The Feelings of Depression

These early warning signs lead us to enter depression where we feel enclosed by its dark walls. These feelings shut us out of others' lives and cause us to be down on ourselves.

We feel the sting of perfectionism as it pierces our sides and leads us into a deeper depression. The waves of negativity infect our thinking in previously unknown ways.

Then, we are unable to see past the negativity. Our minds are clouded with it so that we are unable to cope. It is as if we have been shut out of the light forever.

Those moments of depression are difficult, because they are life-sucking, literally taking our breath away. We can no longer function, so we stay at home. We take off work because we don't want to go out. We don't want others to experience our depression.

Instead, we would prefer to suffer in silence and isolation, deep within ourselves, because we have pride that we can overcome it alone only by entering a profound introspection of ourselves.

My Experience of Depression

In the deep introspection of my life, I have experienced the deep chasm of depression. It is life-altering.

When you are depressed, you can feel it taking every ounce of energy from you and you don't want to go anywhere but remain in the darkness.

But then, you also want to fight for your life to get out. Deep within that self-analysis is an evil spirit that wants you to stay there, that wants you to die and suffer forever. It is a type of hell that people who are depressed experience.

They listen to the lies of this evil spirit, thinking that they will not be able to get out of it; that there is no way out.

Whenever I felt depressed, I had to get out of the mindset that the depression is going to take over my life. In the moments I feel depressed, I remind myself, "You have overcome so much. Before this, you were able to conquer the depression.

Don't think that this moment is any different. Keep fighting. You have to go on. Although you feel that this moment is a time of mourning, tomorrow you will be thriving and dancing!"

The way to deal with depression is to fight. Fight, I tell you, fight! You cannot passively expect to get out of depression.

Don't allow the lies of the evil spirits and demons within it to take over your life. There is nothing worse than allowing those things to cause you anxiety and pain deeper than the depression itself.

Depression is an illness that can only be fought. When you experience it, you have to fight for your life, because truly, at times, it can seem like a matter of life or death.

Depression is a dangerous place to be, but only when you can move beyond the hopeless feelings and low energy can you overcome that place that grieves your spirit.

My journey of fighting through depression started with my diagnosis. Progressively over time, I was able to discover what I needed to do to get better.

Over about ten years, I journeyed through to get to a better place of healing and restoration. I would fell and got back up again many times.

Occasionally, I would be depressed and feel down and want to stay home all the time. I would feel a great weight of pressure that was crushing me. It was suffocating me so that it was so hard to breathe.

The strains of depression can make a person go into a deep chasm within themselves. With God's grace, I have never entered into the chamber of suicidal thoughts that could destroy me forever.

Instead, I have been spared much of the inner demons that can cause a person to fly off the handle because the hopeless feelings of it can overpower and conquer.

My life has been a testament of healing and recovery that has allowed me to come out triumphant over the inner turmoil caused by depression.

Chapter 2

Seeking Professional Help: Psychiatrist and Counselor

In this section, I will talk about how I sought help from a psychiatrist and counselor and was able to get professional assistance for my mental illness.

One of the biggest lies people believe when they have a mental illness is that they have to have it all together. They think they can get assistance without going to a doctor or psychiatrist.

These individuals have a great deal of self-reliance and feel they must face the elements all by themselves. They never bother going to see a doctor to get medicine for whatever ailment is bothering them.

Men are more likely to be this way and are less likely to seek mental health help when they need it most. The rise of male suicides far exceeds that of women in the United States today.

No wonder so many people are not getting the help they need! They aren't looking for it. Instead, they pursue their path without regard to what they need: someone who can listen to and help them.

When I was first diagnosed with depression, I believed I needed someone to help me. I was compliant with my parents and doctors and didn't want to question it.

I knew that doctors and psychiatrists were helping people and that they were the ones who were going to get me where I needed to be.

I trusted them and believed that modern medicine could get me the guidance I required.

Week after week, I went to see a psychiatrist help me with my illness. I had to try different doctors to get it right. There were a couple of terrible doctors who did not help me at all. One of the doctors saw me in the hospital. What was his solution to my problem? Drugs.

He gave me so many drugs that I could hardly function, let alone get up out of bed every day. He was not helpful.

One of our family friends said, "Get away from that doctor. He won't help you at all." So, my parents stopped my appointments. It made a huge difference. Soon, we were able to find a medical professional who made the biggest impact on my life in healing from the disorder.

He was a bit older than others, nearing retirement. But it was amazing to see how this doctor interacted with me.

He was special. You don't normally find this kind of caring, gentle, nurturing, and sensitive demeanor from most physicians, but that's the way he was.

He always smiled at me when I walked into the office and was always willing to listen to me, even when I felt I was going through a difficult time. Dr. S. knew I had high goals for my life.

He knew that I wanted to get into higher education and get a terminal degree in an advanced subject. I told him that I wanted to become a doctor one day and go to a prestigious school.

I didn't want to back down on that goal, although I had a mental illness. I also didn't want to allow my illness to impact my life, because I could not just give up. It was not in my blood.

My family never gave up, so I wouldn't allow a difficult circumstance to deter me. Dr. S. saw how much I was persevering through my last year of high school and he stated that he was proud of me.

He always encouraged me and let me know that I would be able to live a normal life. Dr. S. saw the progress I made, and he knew that

I get better within a year or two, and it was amazing how he got me there.

How did I start recovering? Healing began with medical consultations with my psychiatrist, Dr. S. The doctor tried numerous formulas for medication.

Disclaimer: There is no magical formula for medicine. Everyone has different body chemistry. Each person's body reacts differently to different medicines, and no two persons will be in the same.

I cannot prescribe medication to suit your situation. You must consult a psychiatrist to help you. Dr. S. tried different medications with me. These medicines had various side effects.

Some of the medicines, especially the antidepressants and anti-seizure medications, caused me to feel manic and relapse into symptoms that I had before, so we discarded those.

It took over a year to get where I needed to be. I continued to consult with my doctor when I was in college. During that time that I was able to develop a wellness plan.

My doctor guided me, not just in prescribing medicine, but also in getting me to feel well and do things that encouraged a healthy lifestyle. He always told me to eat a good diet and to exercise, so I did. Dr. S. helped me manage my stress so that I could do all the things I needed to succeed academically.

Seeing my doctor every week was crucial in getting me where I wanted to be. I was not ashamed. I allowed myself to submit to the authority of medical professionals who had much greater knowledge about mental health. It made a difference.

I think a lot of people don't seek medical attention because they are too proud. They think that they can do it alone by reading a self-help book or using another resource. Professional help is a necessity in many situations.

Stop trying to be strong. Seek medical guidance from someone who understands your condition better than you do. Allow them to help you achieve your dreams. It will be one of the best decisions you'll ever make.

Choosing the Right Doctor

Choose a medical professional who will listen to you. Find someone who will hear you out on all the issues you face.

Going to a doctor who only offers advice without listening to you is counterproductive and will not help you. Find a doctor who will listen to what you have to say because your experience of the illness is an important part of your treatment plan.

A doctor should not drug you to the max. There are plenty of physicians who put their patients on as many prescriptions as possible. Avoid them.

Realize that you cannot yield to the authority of someone who will cause you cognitive impairment and irreversible memory damage.

Locate a doctor who will be on-call in case there is an emergency and who will be available when you need them because that will help you endure whatever crisis may arise.

One last bit of advice, stick with the doctor that meets your needs and comes up with a treatment plan that will help you.

Try Talk Therapy

In addition to your psychiatrist, the choice of a therapist is important. In many cases, I would say this is an equally essential consideration.

Often, it is helpful to see a therapist who is of the same gender because that can help ease any communication burdens that may cross those lines.

Talk therapy is a proven method to help with depression and anxiety disorders.

When I was dealing with my depression and anxiety, I went to see a therapist who was also able to help me through those periods and develop positive thinking techniques that helped me out of the difficult thinking I had as a result of depression.

I would say, however, that talk therapy is not an absolute necessity for treatment for depression. Seeing a therapist is something that you can do whenever you feel like it and perhaps only at times of deep depression.

It is not mandatory to see a therapist. There are other ways to get help, including social therapy.

When a person spends time with their friends, they can experience happiness and comfort because they feel that they are with people that understand and love them.

That is important in this world. Having friends makes a difference in how we live. People with depressive illnesses can benefit from having a few close friendships, which can be life-giving and life-changing in the midst of hard times.

They can be a vital source of energy in the middle of the depression, which is a time in which many people choose to close themselves inward.

Emotions and Moods, the Difference

How do you react when something terrible happens, such as getting laid off from work or your business crashes? You feel either sad or angry or both at the same time, right?

Now, how do you classify what you experience? Are they emotions or moods, or maybe both? Emotions and mood may be strikingly similar, but you may be surprised at how distinct they can be.

People, most of the time, use emotions and moods interchangeably. In reality, however, psychologists have made distinctions between these two words.

How do you make the distinctions? One common difference is that the time frame for both is different. Specific or indeterminate reasons usually trigger emotions.

Their outcomes are generally intense but short-lived. On the other hand, the mood often lingers longer than emotions, and it also comes in a milder nature.

It is possible to trace the source or reason for your emotional outbursts, but in the case of mood, you might find it challenging to identify a specific trigger or what caused your mood change.

How Do Emotions Define Us?

Emotions are the mind's preferred tools for controlling our mood and the amount of positive energy available for us to use at a specific moment.

They are one of the primary reasons why the mind is the most powerful organ in the human body. Happy people are happy because they can manifest positive emotions more than negative ones. In other words, it is what you process in your mind that you become. The kind of emotion you carry around on average will determine how you relate with people.

Emotions have the power to create our personality profile and determine behavior toward other people. People with positive emotions are going to find it easier to connect with more people than melancholic people.

You are more likely to patronize the mall with attendants who always wear captivating smiles on their faces than the ones with gloomy-faced attendants. Your emotions create connections with your environment.

Emotions change us

When an emotion is manifested, what do you think happens?

The brain activates the body to fall in line with the emotion. For instance, when you are angry, your heart might start to beat faster.

When you are sad, tears might start coming out of your eyes. In the instance, when you feel happy, you begin to smile. Emotions create some physical reactions in us that we might not even notice.

Your body begins to react differently. You think differently, and you see things from another point of view.

For instance, when you are happy, you might smile at that homeless person and drop a coin or two. But when you are sad, you might not even notice him.

How you see and react to your surroundings is dependent on your emotions.

Memories are triggered. The kind of emotions you are having will determine the memories you will have. Happy people always reminisce happily and enjoyed memories. Disappointed people might go on to start recounting the number of times they have faced the same sad situation.

Understanding your emotions is, therefore, very essential to fashion out the ways to respond to them appropriately.

When you know your emotions, you can create escape routes from negative emotions and quickly and effectively switch to positive ones.

Chapter 3

Essential Emotions to Master

If emotions determine our state of mind, then everyone needs to get to speed with some of the most basic emotions we experience daily.

To be honest, no one is going to enjoy only positive or negative emotions. So, you must learn to remain in the moment, create more positive emotions, and manage the negative ones better.

We will now discuss some basic emotions and how they influence character and behavior.

Fear

Imagine being in a dark room, and all you can hear is strange sounds. Fear creeps in as a signal of survival. Fear is the condition of a recognized threat to safety, comfort, or existence.

When you are in some kind of danger, your body activates a system called the "fight or flight response."

In all cases of fear, the muscles will become tense, your brain is more alert, and your heart rate increases.

Your response level is extremely high, and you are super-conscious of your environment.

When you are experiencing fear, the following expressions are usually noticeable:

- Active response mode to either face or flee the threat scene
- Unusual facial expressions like dilation of the pupils and rapid blinking
- Physiological responses like breathing heavily

Our levels of sensitivity to fear are different. So, we cannot perceive fear in the same way. To some, certain things trigger fear. Trivial fear is often referred to as "trifling fear," while terrible fear can be referred to as "serious fear."

Nervousness and Horror are closely associated with this kind of emotion and can be further related to the following:

- Anxiety
- Worry
- Uneasiness
- Dread
- Distress
- Panic
- Terror
- Shock

What to know

Fear is a reflex protective state that enables us to survive. When we enter fear mode, the body is alert, ready, and able to respond better in most cases. Fear goes beyond physical threats though.

Even when you are scared about events yet to happen or outcomes, it is the same basic principle. However, fear can be debilitating when it is based on unfounded suspicions.

Therefore, fear is a necessary survival reflex but should not be allowed to last longer than needed. It could incapacitate you otherwise.

Anger

Anger is invoked by feelings of hostility, frustration, antagonism, and ill-feeling.

When someone makes you angry, you may be prompted to either retaliate by physical means or storm out of the scene.

Thus, anger like fear also ignites a hyperactive mental state. In, the following expressions are usually present:

- The tone of voice becomes harsh. Often accompanied by yelling.
- Physiological reactions, such as sweating, occur.
- Facial expressions, like the glaring, stern look develop.
- Violent behaviors, such as kicking, hitting.

There can be active and passive anger. In the presence of active anger, you may want to attack the target immediately, either verbally or physically.

In passive anger, the person holds a feeling of hostility against the target and silently sulks.

What to know

Anger is often accompanied by short-lived but powerful emotional surges and energy outbursts.

In periods of anger, you may suddenly develop the strength or motivation to do things you are not necessarily able to do otherwise.

Anger, on rare occasions, can be the precursor of positive outcomes, especially when it forces someone to change or arms you with extra motivation to achieve a goal.

However, anger must be reined in and controlled at every point.

You cannot allow yourself to lose your cool and handover the initiative for controlling your mental state to an external body.

Sadness

Sadness is another powerful emotion that affects and controls your behavior. It is a temporal emotional condition.

The feeling of sadness can be expressed in various ways including,

- Crying
- Loneliness and quietness
- Exhaustion

Sadness is characterized by feelings of Disappointment, Sympathy, Isolation, Dishonor, and Neglect. The continued presence of sadness can bring about depression.

What to know

Sadness is a critical emotion because it happens frequently and can impact your entire mood and actions. In contrast to anger and fear, in sadness, the body's reaction time is slowed.

It is a feeling of helplessness and can make you feel bad and weaker than you are.

No one can eradicate sadness. What you can do though, is to limit the way events and other people affect your moods. A lot of times, we get sad over things that are not even worth it.

Learning to toggle off your sadness can be a key weapon in retaining control over your mind.

Contempt

Once in a while, everyone falls guilty of thinking less of another person. Contempt involves creating some form of imagined or real superiority complex.

Contempt arises in circumstances where you feel the other person is less important, less influential, or intelligent.

In another way, you exercise your contempt towards the other person by acting in ways that tend to intimidate or cause a reasonable apprehension that you dislike the other person. Disgust, Indignation, and Hate are related emotions.

What to Know

Contempt is not a nice emotion, as we all know. Yet, we still fall into its pit more frequently than we know. It reeks of narcissism and arrogance.

Surprise

This is usually a brief emotion and is invoked by a psychological startle. It is a response to an outcome you did not expect.

This expression can be negative or positive. It is negative when you are startled unpleasantly.

For instance, if someone jumps out of the door to scare you as you enter the room. It can be positive when something nice that you weren't expecting happens. Expressions that characterize this emotion include:

- Verbal expressions like yelling or gasping.
- Facial reactions like leaving the mouth opened and raising your brows
- Bodily reactions like jumping

What to Know

Surprise tends to create lasting memories as people are likely to remember unexpected events in their lives.

Happiness

Everyone wants to be happy. It appears that it is the most sought-after emotion. Happiness can be considered as the height of all emotions.

The reason you work is that you want to make money, do the things you love, and be happy. Happiness seems to be the end goal of all human efforts.

The expressions prevalent during this emotion includes positive body language cues such as smiling, relaxed body posture, and general upliftment.

This emotion can come complex to Ecstasy, Delight, Joy, Enthusiasm, and Thrill.

What to Know

We desire happiness every moment of every day. Unfortunately, very few people are deliberate about staying happy. Most of the happiness people enjoy is unpremeditated.

Most times, people get happy after receiving positive surprises.

However, by being deliberate and consciously attuned to what your mind and body are saying, you can stay happy for longer.

Chapter 4

Anxiety Disorders

Before we can even know about the different types of anxiety and effective ways to cure anxiety, it is paramount that we first understand what anxiety is and where anxiety stops being just anxiety and becomes an anxiety disorder.

Anxiety can be described as a normal reaction to stress, which may be beneficial or destructive based on the reaction levels.

This means that anxiety per se is not bad as it helps us to deal with challenging situations. However, if you are too anxious such that anxiety affects your whole life and controls you, then there is a problem.

When simple anxiety becomes a full-blown anxiety disorder, you become constantly worried and have overwhelming worries and fear.

There are many forms of anxiety disorders; hence, we will look at each anxiety disorder for you to understand them further.

Short-Term Anxiety Disorders

Short-term anxiety disorders are exactly what it sounds like—it is experiencing severe depressive symptoms that can last upwards of six months if left untreated.

During this time, people feel as though they cannot get out of bed or function at all. This is perhaps the most extreme form of depression and can be debilitating.

People who face Short-term anxiety disorders are likely to only experience one episode, but others will face several of them.

Without treatment, these are left unchecked and able to escalate.

Long-Term Anxiety Disorders

If the anxiety is caused for the long term, the person usually experiences a host of other experiences. When anxiety is caused due to a single event or so (like writing an examination), it will eventually fade away as the event passes by.

If the reason for anxiety is a tussle between you and your mother-in-law, then it is likely to be caused for a brief period (till whenever you both see each other). Such cases are usually accompanied by other symptoms, including diarrhea, irritability, and constipation.

If the anxiety is caused due to some problem at work, then it is likely to be a long-term problem. You may fear getting up in the morning or going to the bed at night (as you will need to go to work).

You will feel anxious on the weekends (as once it is over you will need to go to work). If the root of anxiety always hangs around, you may experience certain other symptoms chest pain, loss of appetite, loss of sleep as well as sexual desire.

All these situations described above will lead to anxious moments day in and day out. Even though such anxiety is pretty common and part of our everyday life, it impacts our health mentally, physically as well as emotionally.

Generalized Anxiety Disorder

One of the most prevalent anxiety disorders around, Generalized Anxiety Disorder (GAD) is characterized by an excessive worry about almost everything in a person's life with no particular cause or reason as to why.

Individuals who have GAD tend to make a big deal out of everything. They become anxious about everything in their life — are it their financial status, work, family, friends, or health — and are constantly preoccupied with worries that something bad might happen. They expect the worst-case scenario about everything and always try to look at things from a negative point of view.

With that said, it's easy to see how GAD can make it difficult for someone to live a happy and healthy life. It can come as a hindrance to their day-to-day life and become an issue with regards to their work, family, friends, and any other social activities.

Some of the most common symptoms of GAD include excessive worry or tension, tiredness, inability to rest, difficulty sleeping, headaches, mood swings, difficulty in concentrating, and nausea.

Fortunately, however, CBT has worked wonders in treating all these symptoms and more.

With the help of CBT, individuals suffering from GAD can change these negative thoughts into positive ones, which will ultimately change their behaviors for the better as well.

There are several CBT techniques that people with GAD can apply to better manage their symptoms.

For example, if you have GAD and want to feel relief from all the muscle tension in your body, you can try yoga; whereas meditation can help you stop overthinking, and breathing exercises are good to practice when you start to feel yourself getting anxious again.

Yoga has been proven to help lower a person's stress, which in turn, relaxes their muscles as well.

There are several different yoga poses and routines you can find on the internet tailored to relieving your stress and anxiety.

Some examples include the eagle pose, the headstand, the child's pose, the half-moon pose, and the legs up the wall pose.

If you need help getting started with how to use yoga to ease some of the distress you may feel from GAD, here is a quick rundown of how you can do it:

- Go to the gym and sign up for their yoga class.
- Or if you prefer, you can stay at home and do yoga by yourself.
- It's often best to do yoga in the afternoon or at the end of the day, as a way to decompress.
- Set up your mat, and if you want, play some relaxing music.
- Breathe in and out, deeply.
- Be aware of your breathing as you move through each pose.
- Take your time going through all the movements.
- Most importantly, enjoy yourself and keep your mind clear.

On the other hand, if the most problematic symptom of your GAD is overthinking and emotional turmoil, not muscle tension and chronic pain, then meditation just might be the CBT technique for you. Here's how you can do it:

- Download some guided meditation videos online (there's plenty on YouTube).
- Listen to them regularly, preferably every day (as you wake up or before you go to sleep is the most ideal).
- Find a quiet place to do this, where you can be alone and away from distractions.
- Devote all your attention to these 10-30-minute mediations and do not think or worry about anything else while you're doing so.
- Make it a rule that once you start meditating, you need to forget about everything else going on in your life and just focus on the present moment.
- Repeat everything the instructor is saying in the guided meditations

By meditating, you are giving your anxiety a healthy and positive outlet and releasing your physical tension from your body. The more you do it, the more peace of mind you will feel, and the easier it will be for you to overcome your anxiety.

When using CBT, a person with GAD will have a much more favorable perspective in life. Instead of always worrying and thinking about the worst-case scenario, CBT reinforces an optimistic and reasonable outlook on life, which will then have a positive impact on their behavior as well.

Most of the time, they'll change from a tense and edgy person to a relaxed and easygoing one that doesn't assume the worst out of everything.

Chapter 5

Practicing Mindfulness to Overcome Anxiety

In this section, you will be learning how to break yourself loose from the shackles of obsessive worrying and anxiety by taking some time to practice the simple exercise referred to here as "mindfulness".

You see, the ability to think is one of the distinguishing factors that are unique to humans and make us distinct from animals.

This thinking faculty in us is what gives us the power to sustain an idea and make real products and render useful services from it.

This same ability, however, exposes us to a different type of fear that is not known anywhere in the animal kingdom but only in human society. This type of fear is known as psychological fear.

Psychological fear comes from the knowledge of something that has happened in the past and has the possibility of recurring again in the future.

The ability to think recreates a vivid picture of how it happened the last time in our imagination, whether it had happened to us personally in the past or we read about how it happened somewhere or to someone.

Animals do not have this gift of creative imagination and that is why they do not experience the fear attached.

A problem with thinking occurs when you confuse thoughts about things with things themselves.

It's easier to think of an imaginary frog and knows that the frog in your head is not the same as a real frog. But when your mind gives you something physically non-existent, such as your self-esteem, it is difficult to notice the difference.

Everyone has negative thoughts sometimes and may even at a point or another believe them. However, not everyone develops persistent anxiety, depression, or emotional distress.

An important question arises: what controls and determines whether these thoughts will go away, or whether prolonged and intense distress will develop?

You see, thoughts of self-esteem are no more real than an imaginary frog. If you switch to the "be" mode, you will see it much more clearly.

You can distance yourself and observe the thoughts and feelings that come to your mind and leave it like sounds, tastes, and types.

Therefore, when your thought gives out: "I feel like a failure", you should not perceive this as reality and fall into inevitable rumination.

This is not trying to say that animals do not fear, but rather they only experience the fear that has to do with a current event or occurrence.

Birds migrate in large numbers when they notice bad weather approaching, that is fear but unlike psychological fear, it is not based on imagination but the warning of their instinct.

There is another interesting fact about psychological fear. It is the fact that though the event you are thinking about is just a figment of your imagination and not a real occurrence at the moment, the human body responds just as it would have if the event was happening.

Anxiety often results in an uncoordinated state of the human mind and the body, where the thoughts patterns move in one direction, the emotions move on the other, and physical sensations also go in another direction. The life of the person seems fragmented.

Simply put, even though the event might not be happening in the present, the effect is real on the person and ends up scattering or distorting his/her current perception of reality.

When a person is anxious, the mind moves freely and separates from the body and the body ends up suffering the effect of this erratic flow of the human mind.

The thoughts, emotions, and physical sensations vibrate at different "frequencies". The good news, however, is that mindfulness as a tool can help bring balance.

A lot of people get lost in thoughts and the process of thinking has almost become an unconscious one for them.

Mindfulness is a skill that can be learned and developed over time if it is intentionally cultivated by frequent practice.

It may seem difficult to engage in at first, this is because an average mind tends to disperse quickly and get lost in thoughts about the future, and every possible thing that can go wrong.

However, it is a worthwhile engagement considering the effect of our thought on our daily life and by extension, our future.

What does mindfulness have to do with anxiety?

Anxiety occurs when you are focusing attention on all the uncertainties while neglecting other possibilities.

It is not uncommon to find people caught up in what-if scenarios, working with hypotheses and situations beyond their control when it would have been easier to have a better and a more positive outlook rather than the energy-sapping negative thoughts.

Imagine a businessman that has an important presentation before his would-be investors the next day suddenly falling into an unnecessary panic attack.

He will most probably begin to think about everything that could go wrong before, during, and after the presentation. He would never think about so many other good things that could go right.

Thoughts such as forgetting the flash drive, not able to speak properly, the slides not opening on the computer, the problem with the public address system or eventually making a very poor presentation that will not impress the investors, etc.

Mindfulness gives you full control and the mind ends up being a useful tool rather than a troublesome master. It can be willingly engaged, for example, one of the easiest ways to start engaging in mindful thinking is during a meal.

During the process of eating, pay closer attention to the food on your plate, taking into cognizance its colors, textures, flavors, and how it feels when you chew.

This is far better than simply gorging in the food without any particular interest in the whole process. This is how to engage your mind positively.

One great thing about mindfulness is to be aware that you are thinking. Your thought is something you produce willingly and not something that should go on spontaneously or accidentally like a train running without a brake.

When you are engaged in mindful thinking, you will be in charge of your thoughts and reprogramming your thought patterns.

Past thought patterns that had been built through a previous lifestyle, experiences, culture, and core-relationships such as with parents, school, family, and every person who had played an important role in your life and upbringing.

Many of these thought patterns are toxic to your mental health and so must be eliminated by all means.

The 10 Best Ways to Support Someone with Depression

A depressed person needs the support of the people around them, particularly people that the person has close relationships. This can be difficult in depressive illness.

As depressed individuals may withdraw from social activities, express a lack of interest in participating in formerly pleasurable activities, and may build a wall with their significant others that renders communication with them difficult.

At this point, these issues that depressed individuals and their loved ones face are nothing new. The first step is naturally to have the right approach to your partner's condition.

This is a condition that they are dealing with and if you want to help them you may have to occasionally put some of your personal feelings and needs to the side, at least briefly.

This laying to the side of one's feelings and desires can be very difficult for some people. Let's face it. We live in a narcissistic age.

Men and women who watch self-help videos or read inspirational books may be familiar with this idea that if someone is a source of negative energy in your life then you should consider cutting them out. This may seem like a natural thing to do, though it is important to note that this type of thinking is very characteristic of the modern world.

Many families may have had an uncle or parent with a substance abuse problem or someone else who was dealing with a bad marriage or joblessness.

Is the solution to simply cut that person out of your life? Although many people today may see this as something viable and even ideal, it is clear that the institution of the family has been somewhat eroded by the difficulty that modern people seem to have in acting in a truly selfless manner.

Yes, a depressed person may be frustrating to deal with because of their moods and the "wall" they build, but people like this need family more than others. It is not beneficial to these people (or to their families) for them to be cut off because of their dysfunction.

Some of the most talented people in human history suffered from melancholia or depression and you may be tossing a talented person who may one day be beneficial to you and others to the side by perceiving their illness as something inconvenient for you.

So, the point here is that a little altruism goes a long way. By being a little selfless in trying to help your significant other who is depressed you may find that one day someone may behave selflessly toward you in your time of troubles.

That may be a spouse helping you through your depressive illness or someone else helping you through another problem.

Alright, so with that long caveat to the side we can start to talk about how a spouse can support a significant other who is depressed. Some of these tips are straightforward while others may take a little thought to understand fully.

Tip 1. Do not be judgmental.

This first tip may be a no-brainer to some readers. That being said, it is not a no-brainer for everyone which is why it is important to mention here.

Depression is not easy to deal with and that includes the depressed person himself or herself. One of the reasons why there is so much stigma surrounding depression is that many people have preconceived notions about depression. These notions may come from perceptions they have about depressed people they have seen or from misconceptions about why a particular person is depressed.

"Snap out of it" is something that someone may be inclined to say to a depressed person. In the past, a statement like this might have been perfectly reasonable to say to someone who is depressed but now we understand that depression stems ultimately from disorders in brain chemistry so the individual may not be able to snap out of it.

Perhaps the first effective step that you can take toward supporting someone who is depressed is by deciding not to be judgmental. Depressive illness is hard.

This condition looks different in different people and depression does not go away when we project our negative judgments onto depressed people.

Tip 2. Educate yourself about depression first, before you plan your "strike."

In reality, you the reader have taken one of the most significant first steps in supporting someone with sadness. Men and women are often judgmental when it comes to depressed people because they do not know much about depression.

A person who has never experienced depression is sure to have a host of preconceived notions that impact how they perceive depressed people that they meet, even when that person is someone close to them like a partner or spouse.

Therefore, before you even begin to think of a "plan of attack" in dealing with sadness in a significant other you need to first make sure that you have an understanding of depression.

You should understand what depression is, what some of the causes of depression are, what the warning signs are, and how sadness can drastically impact the lives of depressed people and those around them. You would not be reading this book if you did not have some interest in educating yourself on the subject so let the education continue.

Tip 3. Avoid the confrontational, interventional approach.

It is easy to see depression as something dysfunctional in another person's life that simply needs to go away. There are television shows that involve handling dysfunction from what can be thought of as an intervention or interventional approach.

What this means in the context of depression is pouncing or cornering the depressed person (often with other family and loved ones involved) to impress upon the person how damaging their condition has been to themselves and the people around them.

Although this sort of approach may be effective in people with substance abuse disorders, it probably is not the best approach for dealing with sadness in a relationship. Y

our significant other should be someone that you trust and who trusts you.

They most likely are looking to you as someone that they can go to for support, and they may be waiting for the opportunity to broach the subject of depression with you if they have not already.

Confronting them angrily or forcefully with their depression is not necessary and it is potentially damaging. There are other ways to handle this issue, some of which you will learn more about below.

Tip 4. Use simple gestures to show that you care.

Although some readers may approach this book as a weapon in their arsenal to declaring war on depression and winning that war, in reality, a depressed person may simply need to know that you care. Although the war analogy is one that may be apt for the subject of depression when it comes to supporting someone who is depressed it might be better to think of depression as an illness.

Someone who is suffering from an illness does not want to be attacked or confronted.

Sure, you may feel that as you are not depressed that you are perfectly poised to help your depressed partner, but you have to recognize that they are doing things on their own time and they have a right to.

As much as you may want this depression to go away now, it may be that the individual needs some time to come to grips with their depression and to formulate a way of dealing with it.

In this regard, depression maybe likes the grieving process. It is something that people go through and what they may need during this time is a kind word, a card, or some gesture that indicates that you care.

Tip 5. Do not project your perceptions and experiences onto the other person.

Depression is a subjective experience. That is one of the fascinating things about it. Even though we can say that depressive illness results from a chemical imbalance that probably related to concentrations of serotonin, norepinephrine, dopamine, and other neurotransmitters at synapses in certain parts of the brain, we still have to recognize that each depressed person is a unique person with their unique set of thoughts and experiences.

What that means for you is that even if you educate yourself about this condition there will still be aspects of your significant other's subjective experience of depression that are closed off to you.

Just as you have aspects of yourself that other people do not understand so too does your partner have aspects of him or herself that you do not understand. This tip is related to the tip of not being judgmental although it is not the same. You have to be careful as a loving partner not to project your perceptions of depression and why they may be depressed onto your partner. The goal here is not to be Dr. Freud, but to be an effective supporter.

Tip 6. Stay away from tough-love approaches to handling depression.

Just as a confrontational intervention is often ineffective in supporting a depressed person so too is the tough love approach.

In the context of depression in a relationship, the tough love approach may consist of forcibly dragging your loved one out of bed, forbidding them from engaging in some behaviors associated with their depression, or giving them an ultimatum of some sort, such as saying that you will leave if they do not get help.

Although many people reach their breaking points when it comes to dealing with the illnesses of those they love, the goal is to steer your partner in the right direction and to do that supportively.

You do not want to push your partner away by being harsh when they needed you to be kind. We remember how others treat us when we are down and the last thing you want your partner to do is to think of you as the most uncaring person that they had to deal with in their trying period.

Tip 7. Stay away from comparisons to you or to others who have also experienced depressive illness.

There is a lot of baggage surrounding depression. This condition is common. So many people think they understand it.

Some people have experienced being down or low because of a traumatic or saddening event in their life and they may conclude that this is just what depressive illness is: a brief period that weak people experience when something bad happens.

As you the reader have gleaned as you have read this far, depression is a serious condition that can be linked to chemical imbalances in the brain. It runs in families and even some serious medical states like cancer of the brain can cause depression.

Just because you experience being sad when your gerbil died that does not give you a perch from which to compare what your partner is experiencing to you.

If your partner truly has major depressive disorder then they have a serious condition that requires your support. What you or someone you know may have experienced is not necessarily the same as what your partner may be experiencing.

Tip 8. Be careful when it comes to offering advice to the depressed individual.

We all like to offer advice to people that we see going through circumstances that we feel we can relate to, but sometimes we just need to mind our own business.

Sure, a spouse or romantic partner is someone who matters and who we want to see happy and successful, but going heavy on the advice is a can of worms that should be avoided.

You may feel that medication or therapy is the right solution for your partner's condition, but that is a decision that you need to allow them to make.

There is nothing wrong with offering advice. Indeed, sometimes we need a little advice. But perhaps we can summarize this tip by saying that it is important to recognize when your advice or input would be unhelpful in a particular situation.

Remember, the goal here is to support your partner not to force them to do what you think they should be doing.

Tip 9. Avoid shaming people for how they express their thoughts and feelings, including ones that may appear negative.

Sadness can be difficult to understand for people who have not experienced it.

Depressed people may appear defeatist, negative, pessimistic or a host of other words that exist in the English language for people we think are allowing their thoughts to influence their behavior negatively.

Sure, some people are defeatist and negative, but when it comes to depressive illness this is an issue that is more layered than it may appear at first glance.

What you can do to be supportive even when you find the things your partner is saying frustrating and difficult is to be an active listener.

By listening to what your partner has to say you not only gain insight into what they are going through but you demonstrate in a salient way that you have compassion for them.

Compassion is one of the hallmarks of a supportive individual, and this is an opportunity to show how supportive you are.

Tip 10. Help the other person obtain treatment but allow them to make their own decisions.

At the end of the day, if you feel that your partner is depressed, you most likely desire for him or her to obtain treatment of some kind, whether that treatment is in the form of medication or something else.

Although this is a perfectly acceptable desire on your part, you have to recognize that this depression is something that the other person is dealing with and that they need to make decisions on their own time.

They have to decide what the right course of treatment is for them.

Even the decision of when to get treatment is one for them rather than for you.

Being supportive does not have to mean forcibly dragging someone out of the gutter and getting them to do what you think they should be doing. Support entails just that: support.

Let them tell you what their feelings are; let them tell you what their visions for the future are.

Even though you may feel that you know what is best, being supportive means sliding over into the passenger seat and letting the other person take the wheel.

How to Eliminate Negative Thoughts

Negative thoughts may be triggered by a feeling, a memory, or statements made by someone else - but once a negative thought has been sown, it compounds at an alarming rate.

Soon, you are then drowning in a sea of negativity, culminating in anger and anxiety.

Whether you have negativity inside of you, or you are surrounded by it, in both cases, the toxicity leaks into your life and holds you back from success.

If you aim to scale the heights of success, you must be ready to fight away negative thoughts. The following are some tips on managing and ultimately getting rid of negative thoughts.

Try to Look at the Positive Side

When you run into a situation that elicits negative thoughts, you might easily get bogged down by the negativity.

However, never allow yourself to sink to such lows.

Instead, you must look at the brighter side—and no matter how bleak the situation appears, there is always a positive thing about it. You just have to look harder.

The following are some of the questions you will have to ask yourself:

- What's the lesson here?
- What's the good side of this situation?
- What can I do differently next time for a better outcome?

146

By focusing on the positive side of the matter, you get to own the narrative as opposed to reducing yourself into a victim, and you also get to mitigate the damage.

People Don't Care Much about Your Actions or Words

Negativity catches on when people start imagining what others may think of them. But the old hard truth is that people couldn't care less about what you are doing with your life. It's all in your mind.

Other people are busy making survival decisions, taking responsibility for their kids, spouses, jobs, and battling fears of what the world thinks of them.

So, when you come around to the realization that the world doesn't care about you as much as you think it does, you will be in a position to take full control of your life and eliminate negative thoughts.

The funny thing is that just as you are afraid of what the world thinks of you, the person next appears also worried about what the world thinks of them.

Question the Thought

Sometimes, you have to be a little philosophical to win against negative thoughts.

In most cases, a negative thought first sneaks up on you and then balloons into a giant cloud of negativity dripping out every pore of your life.

But if you are an introspective person, you can question the validity of the thought.

Start by asking yourself whether you should pay attention to the negative thought, and if you answer in the affirmative, what do you stand to gain?

When you question a negative thought, you cease being the victim and gain power.

Watch What You Feed Your Mind

In this age of technological advancement, negative energy is only a few taps away. Most people spend their time on phones, browsing the internet.

We are on social media, seeking some attention, and we are on other sites, consuming all manner of questionable data.

If you realize that your negative thoughts stem from your habit of consuming unhealthy media, you have to stop that habit.

Of course, it is not easy to get rid of a habit that had been so entrenched into your system, but if you are serious about improving your life, then you must stop feeding your mind with negative content, and turn to positive things.

Remember, just as there is an overabundance of negative things, there's also too much positive content available on these platforms.

Stop Exaggerating Things

If it won't matter five years from now, then it is not a big enough matter. That should be your attitude.

Thus, when a negative thought pops up, don't blow it out of proportion.

You can take the role of the observer and watch it diminish into irrelevance. But when you notice a negative thought and jump into panic mode, you become susceptible to negativity.

Physical Exercise

When you notice that negative thoughts have started creeping up on you, just put on your training gear and head to the gym.

An intense workout will not only renew your energy but also grant you peace of mind. The negativity will be no more.

When you allow yourself to dwell on negativity, you become trapped, and you lose the motivation to fight it off.

Sometimes, negativity crops up as a way of your brain to alert you of mental strain, and all it takes to get rid of that feeling is an intense workout.

Be Kind

One of the best ways of dealing with our negative energy is to spread around kindness. This helps us feel better about ourselves, and it helps us get rid of that negative feeling.

You don't have to do big things to be kind to someone. Even small acts of kindness, such as buying a homeless person a meal, can help you feel better about yourself.

And once you feel great about yourself, you are in a position to get rid of those negative feelings.

Always ensure that you practice kindness; it will not only alleviate negative thoughts but will also draw people toward you.

List down All the Great Things About Your Life

If you are not careful, negativity can cast a dark cloud over all the good things about your life. It makes you blind.

But you ought to be smarter than that. Always ensure that you are appreciative of the good things in your life. By showing gratitude, you enter the appropriate mindset required to eliminate negativity.

Create a list of all the things that are going on well for you.

This will help you see how great you are blessed. And more importantly, it will boost your determination to get rid of negative thoughts and direct your life into positivity.

Take a Walk

Sometimes, thoughts can be triggered by our environment or the people surrounding us.

And so, it is critical to be vigilant of what or who surrounds us. If you suspect that there's a negative influence around you, then do yourself a favor and pull away.

But instead of brooding in a corner, take a walk down a quiet road. This will help get rid of all those negative thoughts.

Talk Them Out

Sometimes, we develop negative thoughts because we have suppressed an issue. In such a case, it is hard to get rid of the negative thought, unless we agree to tackle the issue and find a solution.

If you have suppressed a certain issue, it is important to find the right person and share it with them. It will leave you feeling relieved.

However, when you suppress an issue, you will be giving your power away, and it will keep you from enjoying your life. Talking things out with the right people makes people trust you.

Reach Out to Your Friends

Great friends are the perfect support system. Negativity is likely to affect your productivity and bring you down.

One of the ways of fighting off negativity is by buddying up with your close friends and engaging in an activity that unites you.

When you meet up with your friends and engage in an activity that you enjoy, you will be able to forget about your negativity, and just have fun. Our experiences play a critical role in manufacturing our feelings. Positive experiences lead to positive feelings.

Also, you can elect to tell your friends about the negative thoughts, and they may give you tips on how to overcome such a challenge. Never underestimate how much your friends understand you.

Stop Having Extremely High Expectations

We don't acknowledge it, but most of us have unrealistic expectations about ourselves and the course that our life ought to take.

What normally happens when things don't go as we expected is that we develop a negative mindset. At this point, we may start to think that the world is out to get us and that people are no good.

In the long run, the act of having extremely high expectations stops us from living an authentic life. Unless we get rid of these expectations, we are unlikely to overcome negativity.

Address the Root Cause

Sometimes, negativity stems from issues that are not immediately apparent. Some of these issues might go back to childhood or a past terrible event that scarred you.

Take a moment to reflect on your life and find out what precisely might be triggering the pattern of negative thoughts.

Once you identify the root cause of your negative feelings, you may address the issue and find a permanent solution.

In this way, you will get rid of negativity and create the life that you had always wanted.

Chapter 6

How to End Anxiety and Panic Attacks Fast?

No matter what kind of role you play in life, the ability to properly control and express your emotions is sure to play a vital role. You also need to be able to understand, interpret, and respond appropriately to emotions that others around you have as well.

Think about how it would be if you weren't able to tell when one of your close friends was feeling sad or when one of your coworkers was mad at you. When you are not only able to express and control your own emotions but also interpret and understand the emotions of others, you are said to have emotional intelligence.

To keep things simple, emotional intelligence refers to your ability to perceive, control, and evaluate emotions whether they are your own emotions or emotions that someone else is feeling.

Some people have high emotional intelligence and can control the emotions that they have in many situations while also responding to the emotions of those around them.

On the other hand, some people have poor emotional intelligence; these are the individuals who will explode at almost anything and barely consider the feelings of others.

Let's take a look at the difference between someone who has emotional intelligence and someone who doesn't.

Our first person is someone who takes life as it comes. They realize that most of the time when things go wrong, it is out of their control rather than seeing it as the world attacking them directly.

They rarely get upset, especially over the little things, and know the proper times to show their emotions. Also, this person responds well to how others are feeling. When a coworker comes and starts yelling at them, they don't respond in kind. They realize that something must be bothering that person and they step up to try and help or correct the issue at the heart of the problem.

When one of their friends is having a bad day, they talk through it and help that friend feel better.

Now, let's look at our second person. This person has a hard time controlling their emotions. When they are upset about something, they will explode at others (whether it is that other person's fault or not), they cry easily, and they may have anxiety.

These individuals will often have the idea that the world is against them and little things, the things that don't matter that much, will set them off.

When it comes to responding to others, this is barely a thought.

They will ignore the feelings of their friends and only process events based on how they are personally affected by them. When someone else is mad at them they think that they are being unfairly treated. The world is against them and everyone just doesn't understand them.

The first person we met is someone who has a high level of emotional intelligence. This person knows how to recognize and control their emotions and can even hone in on some of the emotions of others around them.

The second person has a low level of emotional intelligence. They get upset over everything, probably have no idea why they feel the way they do, and they don't even pay attention to the feelings of others.

Of course, some variations happen between these two extremes, and figuring out your level of emotional intelligence can be important for helping you to improve.

Some people believe that you can improve your emotional intelligence with some hard work. But others believe that this is an inborn characteristic, something that you are born with which makes it extremely difficult, if not impossible to change.

There is probably a grain of truth to both schools of thought. We are all born with a natural level of emotional intelligence which we can then either nurture and improve or let it grow fallow through disuse.

The four parts of emotional intelligence

Four main factors are going to determine your emotional intelligence. These include:

- Perceiving emotions: the first thing that you need to do to understand emotions is to learn how to perceive them properly. This can include learning how to recognize nonverbal signals like facial expressions and body language.
- Reasoning with emotions: the next thing that you need to do is use your emotions as a way to promote cognitive activity. This can be hard at first, but emotions can help prioritize what we are paying attention to and reacting to, and we can pay attention to this to learn something about ourselves.
- Understanding emotions: many meanings can come with the emotions that we perceive. For example, if you observe that someone is angry, you may have to take a step back and see why they feel the way they do. A boss may be mad at you for your work because they got in trouble with their boss, they fought with their wife, and they got a speeding ticket, or for a whole host of other reasons and someone with a high level of emotional intelligence will be able to recognize this.
- Managing emotions: next is the ability to effectively manage your emotions. You need to be able to regulate

your emotions, find an appropriate response, and then respond as an important part of your emotional management.

There are several ways that you can measure your emotional intelligence. Some tests can be done to check on this, but it is also possible to figure out your emotional intelligence and change it through hard work and perseverance.

By learning how to recognize your emotions, what is causing them, and the appropriate response to the situation at hand, you can easily improve your emotional intelligence in less time than you might think.

So why would you want to spend your time working on emotional intelligence? There are quite a few situations in your life where a high level of emotional intelligence can make a big difference.

For example, in the workplace. Employees who have a higher level of emotional intelligence are the ones who perform better because they pick out jobs that they are passionate about, do better with other employees, persuade other people to their ideas, and also avoid conflicts.

Think about how some of these skills could help you in your career, whether you are trying to advance or just stay on top. Everyone could use a brush up on these skills to help them do better in the workplace.

Another crucial area where you will see the benefit of working with emotional intelligence is in your relationships, whether these are with a partner, with your family, or even your co-workers. Each person that you encounter is going to have their feelings and being able to recognize these and respond properly will make it so much easier for you to get along with them.

When conflict does arise, you will be able to keep your emotions in check, preventing a bigger blowout than is necessary no matter what kind of relationship you are trying to work on.

Emotional intelligence is something that everyone can improve upon and there are so many benefits to so. However, it is important to realize that it is also a skill that takes some time to master.

You will not be able to wake up after practicing for a day or two and have total control over your emotions. This is probably something that you will have to work on for quite some time before it becomes a habit.

But when you understand this from the start and work hard to observe, understand, and manage your emotions you will be able to reach your goals in no time.

Common difficulties in using the EMDR method

Q.: I do not have time to simultaneously present an unpleasant picture and move my eyes.

A.: You do not have to think about the picture while you are making eye movements. You focus on it at the beginning, and then you can completely concentrate on the movements themselves and upon their completion return to the picture again.

Q.: I chose one picture for study, but after the first round of movements, another one appeared in front of my eyes, also unpleasant, but connected with a completely different situation. Should I continue to work on the original picture or take on a new one?

A.: In such cases, it's recommended to trust your internal process. If a new picture has arisen spontaneously, it is worth working with it. Exercise it until it ceases to cause any discomfort. After that, return to the originally selected goal with which you started work.

Q.: I do not remember the situation completely. I have only a vague or fragmentary memory.

A.: Absolute accuracy is not required at all. Take in the work that material is available to you at the moment. Even fragmentary memories can be effectively worked out with the help of EMDR.

In some situations, after 2-3 rounds of EMDR, the picture takes on more specific outlines, and additional details that you did not remember before may begin to appear in it. But this is not necessary. When you can't remember the situation completely, pay more attention to the feelings that it causes you.

Q.: After 2 rounds of EMDR, the picture remained unchanged, and the intensity of unpleasant sensations only increased.

A.: This is possible: the process of working through negative information occurs through a temporary intensification of an unpleasant feeling. This is natural and happens when a person tries to keep an unpleasant feeling at a distance from himself.

We have already discussed issues of resistance to feelings and the importance of their acceptance before when we talked about the technique of emotional freedom.

When working with the EMDR method, (similar to working with EFT) it is important not to resist the unpleasant sensations associated with the images that you are working on.

Q.: The intensity of the sensations is too high. When I try to work out the situation, I have such strong feelings that I just can't continue. I am afraid that in this case, I will become even worse.

A.: In such a situation, use the technique of emotional freedom (EFT) to relieve the senses and stabilize your condition.

Perhaps you still have too few resources to work out precisely this traumatic moment. In this case, temporarily postpone work with this episode.

While working out less difficult memories for you, use EFT to learn how to better regulate your current state - all this will allow you to increase your stress resistance resource. After a while, you will be able to return to working out the hardest memories.

An alternative is to seek professional help from a specialist who has experience working with severe emotional injuries.

Chapter 7

How Depression Affects Different Aspects of Your Life

Depression not only affects you, but it affects various aspects of your life, including the people you love. Discovering how your life is affected by depression can be one more step towards making improvements and pushing you towards the help you need.

Many times we lose sight of those around us, the love we have for them, and how they can help us when suffering from depression.

Reminding yourself that you do have people who care and they are willing to be "bothered" by your troubles will help you in your treatment.

You will indeed get into a vortex of limited sight when you are in the midst of depression. This cycle of negative thinking can battle between knowing people will help you if you ask, and being unable to ask.

Perhaps you have had thoughts that they will not be able to help you or understand. Maybe, you have tried to reach out, but their own lives are busy and you feel like you are just in the way.

There might be times when you've thought, "I'm always the one to get a hold of that person(s), so obviously they do not care about me."

Often the other side to the story is that your friends and family do care, but you are right—they are living their life and sometimes that life is just as bad as yours.

Your friends might be battling their depression. It's even happened to me. I was suffering greatly from depression brought on by the loss of a loved one, although that loved one was not completely gone, his mind was due to dementia.

My friends said they would be there but never called. It turned out that one of my friends was suffering from post-partum depression and another had been battling depression for 10 years.

All three of us didn't tell each other of our struggles and battles with depression but tried to keep it all inside. Instead of leaning on those that could help and understand, we all chose to keep it to ourselves and try to deal with it in our way.

The following are some tested practices that can help you overcome depression alongside the counseling of medical practitioners.

- Practice caring for yourself – engage in what makes you happy.
- Engage yourself actively.
- You are taking care of your body matters.
- Keep track of your low mood.

Practice caring for yourself – engage in what makes you happy.

As we grow, there is/are one or more things that will have discovered about ourselves, such as those things or activities either make us happy or unhappy. One of the ways to overcome depression is to figure out what works for you.

List those people, activities, and places that ignite the feel-good emotion in you. You can as well list your daily activities to figure out those once that ignite your happy-mood.

It may be hard to include in the list all the things that make you happy, but try to incorporate the content elements, people, and places in your daily activities.

For example, you might be the type that enjoys music, such as playing the piano, playing games, or watching a movie. When this list is generated, ensure that you schedule a time to observe them daily. By doing this, you may overcome depression.

Engage yourself actively

When you engage yourself in active activities, this will also go a long way to helping you overcome depression. Take a step and join a group or forum. for example, the group may be a community project group, a sports team, or even a social media group or forum that can engage you in a discussion.

The essence of this is to keep yourself engage with positivity so that you can close those little holes that allow mood swings.

If eventually you are not encouraged by any of the old things you used to enjoy, leap of faith and find new ideas that can help you always get on your feet, such as volunteering.

 This will make you break out of unhelpful mood patterns and enhance your bright side.

Caring for your body matters

Good quality sleep is essential when it comes to enhancing body functionality. Remember that depression can result from a lack of sleep. Observing good sleep has been proved to show drastic improvement in people suffering from depression.

Another way of taking care of the body to overcome depression is to eat well – have a proper diet. A nutritious and healthy diet helps in enhancing physical and mental strength, and in turn, helps to improve your mood and increase your energy.

Additionally, your hygiene must be dealt with, such as taking a shower before you go out or dressing up well. This can act as a catalyst to brighten up your day.

As simple as these points mentioned above may seem, they have a positive effect on the outgrowing depression.

Keep track of your low mood

This question comes to you. How can I keep track of my depressed mood? It can be achieved by maintaining a mood diary. From the study, it has proved to help in keeping track of your mood changes.

This will help you sense the pattern of attitude that causes depression in you, and enables you to work on it, know the right cure to use and also know what to tell your mental doctor.

Additionally, when you keep track of your mood, you will know how to handle your day by not allowing your mood to dictate the outcome of your day.

Relationships and Depression

Determining the link between emotion and relationships Taking deeper into your relationship. To take positive action to strengthen your relationship. The results of your actions.

Even if we say, we're not at all social. People tend to have friends and family with whom they talk, even if they just talk about a trip to buy food. We work better with support.

Our moods improve, and our ability to cope with stress also increases. It should, therefore, be obvious that all the relationships we encounter somehow affect us, from relative strangers to close friends and families.

Taking the time to improve every partnership will improve your mood and make you feel very relaxed.

You will learn how to strengthen relationships and how to use these strategies more and more. More importantly, we shall examine intimate relationships as they have the greatest consequences for our mental health and learn to cope with the loss of a relationship, which often causes anxiety or despair.

The deep relationships you have are often able to deal with this side of you. Their love demands that they help you work through the troubles, at least for a time.

Those who love you want the best, they want to be able to fix your problems, but their problems can start to stack up. They can begin to affect the person, so they are unable to help you.

If it gets to be too much or you are too unwilling to seek help, then the loved one may pull away. They may try to seek happiness elsewhere or simply give up on you. The strength that exists in your relationship will determine whether a person is willing to stay by your side, through the tough times and provide the care you need.

Some relationships are not strong enough. Sometimes divorce or avoidance is the only way your loved one can handle the depressive state you are in.

People tend to seek happiness when surrounded by unhappiness. They don't want to feel as sad and depressed as you. If they struggle with their depression, then they may also pull away.

Since depression often means sleeping a lot, stopping the hobbies you used to love, and having a lack of concentration, relationships are often the first to be harmed.

A person with depression may refuse to do anything that used to be enjoyable, leaving the one in the relationship without depression to wonder why the person is pulling away. It is a cycle that can injure relationships forever.

The one truth is that the person you love does not want to pull away. They do not want to seek a different relationship, but at some point, they are going to realize that they are either enabling your depressive state or they are unable to help you because it is hurting them.

A caregiver, even one that loves you and is there for you, has to take care of themselves and their needs before they can help you.

Health

Relationships are not the only area of your life to suffer. Medically, your mind is a powerful tool capable of many things, including making you sick. Depression may be a manifestation of your negative emotions, but it can be expressed in severe, chronic pain.

If there is no underlying health condition causing your depression like thyroid disorder, you can make your back, head, or your entire body aches. You can make yourself feel ill, as if you have some horrible disease, and yet have depression.

This pain makes you want to ignore the fun things you use to do in life. You might even wish to lay in bed all day because of the pain and yet, this will not provide a release of the pain.

Depression can also bring on IBS symptoms. Perhaps irritable bowel syndrome is more prevalent because of the high rate of depression. This is unknown, but one thing is for certain—when you suffer from depression your insides suffer.

People with depression have reported IBS with diarrhea. Their stomach becomes so upset, it gets nauseous and requires many bathroom trips. Each time you have this issue, you are hurting your body even more. You can start developing ulcers and hemorrhoids.

Work

Work is greatly affected, whether you show up or not. First, if you do go to work or speak with co-workers when you telecommute, you are often negative. You also tend to avoid doing your job. If you have deadlines, you start missing these deadlines. The quality of your work suffers, and eventually, you are seen as not performing your duties correctly. This can lead to you losing your job.

If you admit to the depression, then you have an out, but only for a short time. Your boss or bosses will only care for a short time that you have a problem.

They will still want to see you returning to a proper performance level. Depression can also be a hindrance for you going to work at all.

There are times when a person with depression calls in sick or requests more time off than they are paid for.

These constant call-ins usually lead to attendance issues, and companies tend to have a policy of "excessive" call-ins.

You can be put on notice that one more missed day in a certain period will be the end of your job.

Tips on Overcoming Anger & Anxiety Issues

To overcome your anger and anxiety problem, you ought to work on yourself with a holistic approach. The following tips are critical in getting rid of anger and anxiety.

Positive Affirmation

Positive affirmation is the act of reinforcing a particular belief into your subconscious. This method is effective many times. It helps an individual develop a strong belief that they can achieve their goal.

For instance, if you intend to win an elective seat in your firm, you can recite certain statements over and over to cement the idea that you are a winner into your subconscious.

Most of the time, we sabotage ourselves because we seem to think that we are undeserving of success—and such an attitude keeps us from making use of our full potential. Most of us are held hostage to negative thoughts that always have distorted reality and caused us to be insecure.

One of the biggest triggers of negative thought patterns is abuse. If a person survived abuse, particularly in their childhood, they are likely to struggle with negativity in their adult life.

Affirmations are an excellent way of overcoming negative thought patterns and making your dreams come true. You have to come up with statements that you must repeat over and over to align your subconscious mind with your goal.

The following are some traits of positive affirmations

They can only influence your behaviors and attitudes: some people try to influence the thoughts and actions of other people through positive affirmation, but they end up hitting a wall.

When it comes to positive affirmations, you can only control your actions and thoughts. Thus, the statements should be guided toward yourself.

But even though you cannot change someone's mind or actions, you can change your response toward them.

They should be simple: affirmations should be simple statements with descriptive words. Some people might have a hard time repeating a phrase over and over again if it appears "hard."

But crafting a simple statement ensures that you won't have a hard time saying the statement.

They must be positive: it is vital to have a positive outlook as opposed to a negative outlook.

For instance, if you want to advance in your career, you may have a positive affirmation like, "I have won the interview" instead of, "I have not been passed over in the interview."

Ensure that your affirmations have a positive connotation. In the present tense: affirmations ought to be in the present tense.

This elevates your mood and helps your subconscious work toward making your dream come true. Thus, you should say, "I have the job," instead of, "I will get the job."

They ought to be full of emotions: your subconscious mind is particularly receptive to emotion-laden messages. Thus, you must ensure that your statements have some emotional weight.

To achieve this, you have to select your words and phrases a bit more carefully. By tapping into your emotional side, you will be motivated to accomplish your goals.

To reap the rewards of affirmation, you have to repeat them consistently. Most people who fail to succeed with affirmations are just noncommittal. And honestly, saying a positive phrase once every three days won't get you anywhere.

But when you repeat affirmations as frequently as you can, you will be in a position to make your dreams come true.

Here are some tips for practicing positive affirmations:

1) Accompany a positive statement with a natural image

One can make a positive affirmation in a silent voice, but to make it more effective, they ought to accompany it with a natural image.

For instance, if you want to attract financial success, it is not enough to merely state your wish, but you also have to dream up a natural image that represents abundance, for instance, a starry sky.

When you learn how to mix these two aspects, you stand a much better chance of accomplishing your goals. To come up with appropriate images to accompany your positive affirmations, ensure that you are in a relaxed state.

02) Soak in the energy of your goal.

Some people imagine that positive affirmation is merely about repeating a statement without engaging other parts of the mind.

They are dead wrong. To make the best out of positive affirmations, one has to engage all their senses. And this is achievable only through active imagination.

For instance, if you are looking for a job, once you make a positive affirmation, use your mind's eye to see yourself having that job.

Assuming that you want to work for a media house as a journalist, paint an image of yourself with a microphone, reporting on the ground.

Living out the experience of a journalist in your mind will speed up the manifestation of your goal.

03) Write an affirmation letter

You might find that your mind wanders off when you try to focus on a goal. You can mitigate this scenario by writing an affirmation letter.

In this letter, you have the opportunity to outline various things and precisely what you want out of life. Some of the letters you can write include:

- Write a letter to the universe outlining the things that you want to manifest in your life and how you aim to improve the world.
- Write down the things that make your ideal day from morning till sunrise.
- When you fail to achieve a goal, write yourself a letter pointing out the factors that have hindered you from achieving your goals.
- Write a letter to someone that you hold in high esteem explaining the qualities about them you admire and wish to gain yourself.

04) Utilize your creativity

You can infuse your creative juices into your positive affirmations and hasten the manifestation of your important life goals.

For instance, you can come up with images, drawings, and music that will add energy to your positive affirmations.

For instance, you can put up an image of your goal on the wall, so that every time you look up, it will reinforce your positive affirmations and bring you closer to your goals.

You may also compose soothing music with lyrics that speak to your dreams. Once you put on that music, it will boost the potency of your positive affirmations. You may put the file into your phone and have it play at a small volume throughout the day.

05) Use the power of smiling.

Positivity is vital when it comes to affirmations. And the subconscious pays attention to our mannerisms and body language.

A scowl indicates negative energy, but a smile indicates positive energy.

Thus, putting on a smile will boost the energy of our positive affirmations and accelerate the achievement of our goals.

Not only does smiling improve our mental status, but it also invites cooperation from other human beings.

When you are struggling with a particularly negative mindset, smiling will help clear negativity, and get started on a positive mindset.

06) Enhance your environment.

Recognize that positive affirmation is to an extent a spiritual exercise. You need a ton of peace and tranquility to realize maximum rewards.

Can positive affirmations be practiced in a chaotic area? Of course, yes. But you will get better results when you practice positive affirmations in a calm area filled with elements of the natural world. Thus, you may do well embellishing your environment.

For instance, eliminate the clutter, reduce machine-noise, put flower vases at the corners, and enhance the natural light falling into your room/office. When you have a serene environment, it will boost the potency of your spiritual exercise.

07) Utilize the natural world.

Nature emits high-frequency vibrations, and without question, it is one of the best environments to practice positive affirmations. If time allows, you can visit an area rich with natural elements, and soak in the splendor of nature.

Take a walk through the narrow paths of a jungle as the trees tower above you and then start your positive affirmation exercise.

Considering the reality of modern existence, being surrounded by nature is not in the cards for everyone, but you can purpose to do that when your schedule allows.

08) Meditate.

Meditation is the act of calming the noises of your mind. We are commonly surrounded by so much activity, and it seeds unwanted energies in our minds.

Meditation is the art of restoring our minds into a state of calm and peace. We achieve this by moving to a quiet area and focusing on positive thoughts while we get rid of our negative thoughts. Thus, when you combine meditation and positive affirmation, you accelerate the manifestation of your goals.

Conclusion

At the end of the day, what is crucial is your wellness. Maybe you are enduring a depressive episode now and need help. Go and seek the help you need. Don't procrastinate any longer.

Find a doctor who can give you the medical advice necessary to manage your symptoms. Sometimes we may need medication to help our bodies get back on the right track. In many cases, we may have to go on medication for the long-term.

That does not make us weak or unable to handle things. Instead, it demonstrates maturity and proactivity, which are necessary to live a successful life.

Find someone you can talk to about your depression. That may be a counselor or therapist or a trusted friend that you can talk to about any matter. In any case, you must find someone who can listen to you and your concerns.

Don't try to do it yourself any longer. Receive the assistance that could save your life. It is the most important thing you can do for yourself today.

What good habits are for battling negative mental states? For almost all of them to be successful, you need to ensure that you practice them regularly which means that your basic life habits are in order as well.

Sleep better: Sleep does wonders for the human body, but too much or too little leaves us unable to think clearly. Our reaction time slows and our memory clouds.

This is to say nothing of the lack of energy that naturally results from too much or too little sleep. All these things drag us down and worsen anxiety. The cure is balance. Doctors recommend that adults get seven to nine hours of sleep a night. Of course, anxiety makes it difficult for us to sleep. Beyond using the exercises we've already gone over; better sleep helps you fight back. There are quite a few things you can do to achieve this end.

Loads of sleep studies have shown that when we use electronics can disrupt our sleep. The effects of light from monitors and television screens affect our bodies much longer than we'd normally think.

A good sleep hygiene practice is to unplug from screen time an hour before bed. It may also improve your mood all around if you're an avid user of social media: studies have shown that those who use social media frequently feel more isolated, even in actual social settings.

Your sleep may also improve simply because you'll be processing less information before hitting the hay. This is particularly true for news junkies.

To make good sleep habitual you need to set a schedule so your body knows what to expect when. The amount of sleep is just as important as when that sleep takes place.

Set a specific time when you'll be in bed and when you'll get out of bed. The latter is easy: use an alarm. In time you'll wake up before the alarm even goes off.

The latter can be harder to accommodate depending on your living situation.

But if you're willing to make the changes it will pay off. On a similar note, try spending less time when you're awake in your bed itself.

A strict sleeping schedule will allow you to be tired when you are supposed to and wake up feeling refreshed. You want to pick a time that you can have about nine hours of undisturbed sleep for example 10 pm to 7 am.

You want 9 hours because it may take an hour for you to fall asleep. If anything comes up that is not urgent and involves you ruining your sleep schedule then decline it.

Some sleeping schedules may also be reversed and this can cause a lot of problems. The problem with this is that you will only be awake during nighttime and most people are awake in the daytime so you will not be able to make plans with your friends and other important things.

Unless you have a job that requires you to work overnight shifts then you should try to fix your sleeping schedule immediately.

Three different methods work best for resetting your sleeping schedule these methods will also work if you're sleeping pattern is just off by a few hours and you want a quick fix.

The first method is to stay up until you are scheduled to sleep. This may be difficult because it involves you being awake for over 24 hours, but if you can handle it then this is the fastest method.

The next method is also pretty difficult because it involves not getting adequate rest for one night and continuing throughout the whole day until you are scheduled to fall asleep.

How this works is that right before you fall asleep you want to set an alarm to wake you up in three or four hours. Once you wake up you must stay awake for at least 16 hours before you fall asleep.

By doing this you are reversing your regular sleeping schedule by four or five hours and once you are on track you can start having a full night's sleep.

This last method takes the longest but it is also the easiest out of the three. It's easier than the other two methods because it doesn't require you to stay up for hours and hours with little sleep.

To do this method you want to either try going to bed one or two hours earlier or later than what you are used to.

So, say for example you usually go to bed at 1 am and you wake up at about 9 am, and your goal is to be in bed by 8 pm and wake up at 5 am.

The first day you do this method you go to bed two hours earlier than what you used to so, in this case, it would be 11 pm. Then the next day it would be 9 pm.

Then from here, you can just go to bed an hour earlier to make it 8 pm which is your goal. Depending on how far your original sleeping schedule is compared to your goal will determine how long this process may take.

Having confidence is about being able to put one step in front of the last without doubting that step.

It's about knowing that what you do in your life is your choice and knowing that no one else can make those choices for you. Don't live by other people's standards. Create your own.

The most important thing that you can take with you from this book is the following, which is based on a practice called mindfulness:

- Yesterday is gone – You cannot change it and it doesn't count anymore.
- Tomorrow has not yet arrived – worrying about it won't help it to be better.
- This moment in life is all that you have.

It's perfectly astute and correct to assume that this moment within your life may be all that you have.

Thus, learn to embrace it and stop feeling bogged down by other people's judgment of you.

If you made mistakes in the past, don't make them at this moment, and don't waste this moment by letting your thoughts drag you into the past. If you can make things right with people by apologizing, do so. If you can't, learn from the mistake and don't make it again.

Depression can go away, but you have to understand that a thought that you have today isn't' important in the overall picture of life. If you waste this moment on negative thoughts, you go into the next moment with negativity already there in your life.

If you fill this moment with positive action, you reinforce your value and you move forward into the next moment as a better person than you were a moment ago.

Thus, it follows that building up your confidence should be done moment by moment. I made a friend a cup of coffee because I knew that she was lonely. It made her feel better. It made me feel better.

Small gestures that take selfish thought out of the picture help to build up positivity that helps to pull you out of the pits of depression. I helped a lady with her shopping because she was older and struggling.

When you give, give with no expectations of return because that's the kind of giving that helps you to build up your confidence in yourself.

You do things because you know they are positive things to do. You don't do them for thanks or something is given in return. When you incorporate giving into your everyday life, it's a positive reminder to yourself that you have value.

Even after a great loss in your life, you need to feel that value explained above. You may lose your purpose for a while, but if you make this your aim in life, you begin to feel you are building strong roots that will take you through all the pitfalls of life with your head held high, knowing that your strength and roots will help you through the bad times that come into your life.

Depression is a phase. It's a stopping point to reassess who you are and make yourself even stronger and more confident, taking you back up the path to happiness.

page intentionally left blank

page intentionally left blank

Self-Love

Transform Your Mindset, Build Self-Compassion, Strengthen Your Self-Worth and Achieve the Life You Desire

Howard Patel

Self-Love

Written by Howard Patel

First Edition

Copyrights Notice

Limited Liability

Please note that the content of this book is based on personal experience and various information sources.

Although the author has made every effort to present accurate, up-to-date, reliable, and complete information in this book, they make no representations or warranties concerning the accuracy or completeness of the content of this book and specifically disclaim any implied warranties of merchantability or fitness for a particular purpose.

Your particular circumstances may not be suited to the example illustrated in this book; in fact, they likely will not be. You should use the information in this book at your own risk.

All trademarks, service marks, product names, and the characteristics of any names mentioned in this book are considered the property of their respective owners and are used only for reference. No endorsement is implied when we use one of these terms.

This book is only for personal use. Please note the information contained within this document is for educational and entertainment purposes only and no warranties of any kind are declared or implied. Readers acknowledge that the author is not engaged in providing any kind of medical, dietary, nutritional, psychological, psychiatric advice, nor professional medical advice.

Please consult a doctor, before attempting any techniques outlined in this book. Nothing in this book is intended to replace common sense or medical consultation or professional advice and is meant only to inform. By reading this book, the reader agrees that under no circumstances is the author responsible for any losses, direct or indirect, which are incurred as a result of the use of the information contained within this document, including, but not limited to, errors, omissions, or inaccuracies.

Table of Contents

Introduction

We all feel down in our lives every once in a while. We do everything we can to make ourselves feel happy and comfortable with our lives. But even with all that, it is still a challenge to try and make our lives as great as they could be.

It is a necessity for all of us to think about the things we can for improving our lives and making them feel stronger and better. This guide is all about helping you to understand what you can do to give your life a greater sense of purpose.

It is especially critical for you to look into what you can do to restore your life and give your self-esteem the boost it needs.

When you feel better about yourself, your life becomes a little easier. You will not try and make things all the more challenging than they have to be. You will certainly feel confident about who you are without dragging yourself down any paths that might be harmful or dangerous.

Your emotions will also be easier to control when you have the self-esteem you require. You will not feel as though you are letting yourself or other people down.

It will be easier for you to have better relationships with other people as well. The general public prefers individuals who feel positive about themselves. They want those who are ready to do anything and are not afraid of themselves.

More importantly, you will feel happier about yourself when you have enough self-esteem in your life. There is no reason why you should feel upset with your life. As you are improving upon your attitude for life, you will find that it is not all that hard for you to get the most out of your everyday experience.

Avoiding Comparisons

One of the greatest reasons why so many people struggle with their lives is because they are constantly trying to compare themselves with others. Some like to compare themselves because they want to think that they are as good as others.

It is natural for all of us to compare ourselves to other people.

We all have our heroes or idols that we love to follow. But sometimes we get far too caught up in those things. We start to think far too much about people and what they are like.

We all like to compare ourselves with all of these people because we think they are all better than us and appealing in some way.

But when we do this, we struggle to look at the big picture.

It only takes a few thoughts or observations of other people to start getting the wrong idea over what can be done in life to make it stand out.

But the truth is that you cannot compare yourself to other people all the time. Think about it for a moment. Let us say that you like to play baseball. You want to try and build your skills up to where you can be the next big-name baseball player.

But no matter what you do, you might struggle to be a big star. You might try and work yourself to death just to try and make it onto a particular team.

It can be difficult to think about how you are not as good as baseball as other people are. That does not mean that you should be comparing yourself all the time.

Not everyone who plays baseball can hit a ball as hard as Aaron Judge. Most certainly cannot throw a ball as fast as Max Scherzer can. They might not be able to make the smartest managerial decisions like Mike Matheny or Joe Madden could.

More importantly, you will feel as though you are not willing to let yourself be who you truly are if you compare yourself to others all the time.

You will not feel all that comfortable with who you are in general when you keep on comparing yourself with others in some way.

Simply put, you have to stop comparing yourself to other people all the time. Everyone has their strengths. You just need to think about yours.

Chapter 1

Nurturing Self-Love with Daily Practices

We should not always expect to rely solely on external sources of love, and that is where the notion of self-love comes in.

A person who practices self-love will never depend on others for his happiness, and it is an inspiring feeling to be happy on the inside. It is about putting yourself first and not being too harsh on yourself. Moreover, as mentioned above, self-love is certainly not about being self-centered and narcissistic.

In this chapter, we will discuss different ways to achieve the power of self-love with daily practices. Let's start:

Eliminating Comparison

As a human as any other emotion is the desire to compare oneself to others. It is natural for us, particularly considering the nature of how most of us are raised and the competitive society in which we live, to compare ourselves to others and our past selves.

Negative comparisons, though, may have a significant effect on our self-esteem, our relationships, our jobs, and our overall life experience.

The irony is that almost everybody feels inadequate in some aspects, and we sometimes wrongly think that if we only earned more money, lost some weight, gained some weight, had a better career, had more friends, moved to a nicer location, met the "perfect" partner or turned our partner into the "perfect" person, had more "success," or something, than these depressed and unhealthy feelings of superior or inferior comparison would just go away. Through coping with it explicitly and getting to the source, we can turn our negative comparison into an experience of development.

To unhook yourself from a negative comparison, here are a few things you should do:

1. **Focusing on Strengths:** Everyone has multiple strengths and limitations. In our unique way, we are all special. Perhaps not all of us were born to be Albert Einstein or Winston Churchill, but we still have the attributes that separate us from others. Sometimes in a big way and sometimes in a small way.

   The concern is that if we are focused on others, we will never be able to see that. If you begin to compare and compete against others, you are more likely to compare yourself to their strengths, even though that very thing may also be yours. So, how is that fair?

You have a unique insight assisted by distinctive insights and unique talents, whether you are a singer, writer, musician, landscaper, or student.

You can respect, serve, and participate. In your little part of the world, you have got everything you need to do well.

Get intimately aware of your previous achievements with the chance directly in front of you and see in the inspiration to try more.

Turn your head back towards the mirror. Here is who you should be comparing yourself to. Find and focus on your strengths.

2. **Turn Comparison into Inspiration:** Although comparing oneself to someone is harmful, learning from the behaviors of others can be very beneficial.

   Habits can be modified, and inspiration can be sought in others. Humbly ask the people you admire or review biographies as inspiration for questions. But if the contrast of your life is a consistent pattern, note which behaviors trigger positive change and which result in adverse impact.

3. **Do not get Attracted by Shiny Covers:** Being conscious and understanding that you do not see the whole story is crucial. We only see what they want to bring out there as we equate ourselves to others. Everybody represents himself in a specific way.

It would usually lead you, as described above, to equate the worst of yourself to the best of others.

Take a minute to reflect on what you put out there for the world to see if you are not too sure about this argument.

It is not about faking it, but it is probably about most people filtering their lives. They very carefully chose what glimpses of their lives they reveal as well as what they mask.

Maybe other people do not know your problems; so, how can you know much about the struggles of the person you have been comparing yourself to?

We live in a time where all share a perfect second in their imperfect day, and we view the perfect second as a life of greatness.

The truth, though, is much different. When we equate ourselves to the achievements of someone else, we see just the outcomes, not the effort.

Your origins cannot be compared to their finishes. You may have been on this journey for just a couple of months, and they have been on it for years.

I think you now have some knowledge of how to live for individuality.

Leaving Judgment of Others Behind

We all want to be loved and respected for our multiple talents, our ferocious intellect, our good humor, our dazzling personalities. After all, in communities where fitting in and getting the confidence and respect of our peers are the indicators of achievement, we have adapted to survive better.

But the need takes center stage often, and what others think of us becomes more important than what we think of ourselves.

We may examine any look and phrase that comes our way for hints that we have been judged and considered appropriate or inadequate.

We get into trouble as we begin to rely on what other people think about us, and we find their opinions vital to our progress. We start tailoring our lives to fit others' needs, and it is a vicious spiral from there.

We miss out on who we are as we surrender our power to others and cause their perceptions to become what we experience. The only truth that we can see is how we think we are viewed by others. Here's how you can change that:

1. **Know Your Values:** You do not have to focus on what the other gym-goers say of you if you admire perseverance and courage, and you turn up at the gym even though you are anxious.

    If you prioritize inner peace and you have to say "no" to someone who asks for your attention, and your plate is already packed to the fullest, you can do so without feeling like they are going to judge you as an egotistical person.

    If you respect honesty and you express your opinion in a crowd, you should do so in confidence, recognizing that you are practicing your beliefs and being yourself. Know your fundamental values and abide by them.

2. **Take Ownership of Your Feelings:** When we base our emotions on the views of other people, we allow them to govern our lives.

We encourage them to be our marionette maker, and we either feel good or bad as they pull strings just right. You feel bad if anyone avoids you.

You may think that by avoiding you, "she made me feel this way." But the fact is that she does not influence how you feel. She has ignored you, and you have given that meaning to the gesture.

To you, it meant you were not worth her attention or you were not nice enough, wise enough, or smart enough.

Because of the meaning, you added, you feel depressed or angry. You have an intuitive response to your thoughts.

We give up the power of our emotions as we give ownership of our emotions to others. The fact of the matter is that you are the only one who can harm your feelings.

You just need to change a thought to change how other people's acts make you feel.

Often this move takes a bit of effort because our emotions are typically automatic or even at the unconscious stage; so, it may take some digging to find out whether the feeling is triggered by thinking.

3. **You Know the Best for Yourself:** No one is going to be as invested in your life as you. You just do what is right for you, and that means learning about your own decisions.

   The only way you can ever understand is to make your own mistakes, to take complete responsibility for them because that way, if you lose, you will at least learn from it sincerely, as opposed to blaming someone else.

Depending on others' judgment can be equal to being a slave to others. The next topic is a severe extension of being trapped in judgments.

Letting Go of Toxicity

In this world, we only have a finite amount of energy and time. So, we must channel that energy into things that matter to us and make us feel satisfied and optimistic.

When the negativity from a dysfunctional relationship gets too much, it drains away all the energies that you might otherwise bring into some more fruitful place of your life that you will never get back.

And if in your life, you are still facing your stress and issues, the unnecessary extra stress can be a massive burden.

That is why it is so important that you chose who you let into your life carefully and spend your time in it. If this person can no longer offer positivity and light, if they merit a place in their lives, you need to think long and hard.

In the past, letting go of stuff has all to do with learning how to move on from the most demeaning of cases. Maybe it is letting go of a poor parent relationship or letting go of self-blame.

Putting Yourself First

The majority of us are told from an early age that being selfless is a positive thing. You are a real person who, much like anyone else, wants to be loved with great care. You deserve to be loved as much as you love someone in the same way. Moreover, no one except you is going to get you where you want to go. Nobody else would if you do not do so.

You need to take ownership of your life and do the things required to get you from where you are to where you want to be if you want to build the life you want. Setting goals and meeting goals take a great deal of effort and attention.

You will quickly get overwhelmed if you do not treat it properly. The desire for self-care, that is, the need to put oneself first, is one of the most neglected aspects of objective accomplishment.

To place yourself first is to ensure that your emotional and physical well-being is looked after by you. Let's get into the ways to do just that:

1. **Learning to Say "No":** If you want to start putting yourself first, the most important thing you need to do is to learn how to say no. It is not that saying "no" means you are arrogant, disrespectful, or unkind. They are all unhelpful assumptions that make it difficult to say no.

   It could feel extra hard to think about how to say no if you are someone who has practiced caring for others. You are used to worrying about other entities and making sure that everything is all right. This is a perfect gift that you are giving to the people of your life.

   However, you need to be sure that your needs are fulfilled to be able to continue giving your caring service to other people. A significant ingredient of self-care is learning how to say no.

   Having healthy limits will allow you to continue to care about others without losing yourself in the process, with the physical and emotional reserve. If you say yes to anyone when you do not necessarily want to, that could lead to frustration that could have a detrimental effect on the relationship. It shows respect for yourself and the other entity to say "no" when that is what you mean because you are honest and genuine, traits that nurture stable relationships.

2. **Prioritizing:** People often misinterpret what "put yourself first" entails. It does not mean doing all the time what you want to do. It does not mean overlooking others' needs. It is just a matter of priorities and learning the relationship between having to take care of yourself and others.

3. **Reminding Yourself "You are important":** You need to constantly remind yourself that you are worthy and important.

   Listen to your requirements, to your needs, to what your heart tells you. If you are out of control, whether you sense like anything is wrong, whether you realize that you do not offer yourself enough, whether you recognize that you want to lead a healthier life, just do not know why you have not begun or cannot commit to it, this is your heart asking you that you are not moving down the road that you honestly want.

I hope now you have understood why it is so important to put yourself first and how you can learn to do it bit by bit.

Living by a Purpose

We do not get burnt out because of what we do. Because we forget why we do it, we get burnt out. The fuel that keeps us alive is the purpose. The problem is that many individuals do not know what their purpose is.

When we look for opportunities to be of value to others and make the world safer, we feel a sense of meaning. Keep faithful to it until you have found the will and purpose for your life.

Do not let someone distract you or talk you out of it. Keep oriented. While walking this path, follow your instincts, for no one has ever walked it before you.

In every way, you are special. Let's discuss some points to guide you in finding your purpose and then sticking to it:

1. **Exploring:** We are all born with a fundamental and positive intention that we must explore.

   Your goal is not something that you have to make up for; it is already there. To build the life that you desire, you must reveal it.

   By investigating two things, you will begin to explore your passion or your intent:

   o   What is that thing you love to do?

   o   What comes to you easily?

It takes time, of course, to grow your talents; even the most skilled artist always needs to practice, but it should feel normal, like paddling downstream instead of upstream.

2. **Persistence:** The pathway to success is never beyond you. You have to keep your dreams intact to keep going forward as you face roadblocks and losses.

   In the last mile, marathon runners should not stop unless they can see the end in sight. And if at that point they are the most mentally weary, they do not give up, and they have a view of where they are heading.

   It is also, indeed, crucial to realize that you are not supposed to be characterized by failure. It is meant to polish you and make you into what you are supposed to be. Roadblocks are part of this ride. There will be no victory without sacrifice. There will be no feeling of satisfaction and victory without losses.

3. **Retain Clarity:** You should be concerned about the legacy that you want to leave behind. It lets you determine how to live now by understanding how you want to be remembered.

   And it is easy to make choices if you know what you stand for and what is important. You can also keep in mind your core. It is about the message that you are going to share.

It is the people that matter to you the most. It is the work that is vital to your growth and success.

Let's move onto our last and most important of staying in the rhythm of realism.

Being Realistic

One of the most exalted characteristics of our time is positivity.

Though it is an admirable quality, everything in excess is bad.

We look up to a person who is always upbeat and enthusiastic about everything, and it always seems like the secret to being happy, prosperous, and well-adjusted is to be a positive person.

Our generation is obsessed with being optimistic because of this, and there are numerous books and podcasts, and posts devoted to a positive thought. But it doesn't always work.

Good thoughts will potentially seriously restrict your achievements.

Being positive is a wonderful idea, and you should definitely do your best to be a positive person, but when it comes to reaching goals, you should instead strive for practical thinking.

I have listed below some ways to develop a realistic approach:

1. **Take Time:** Most people want to push everything, get everything done right now, and be successful with everything they do instantly.

   Most do not find it to be like this, and it takes time for things to happen or to understand.

   The journey of life tells us that almost everything takes time, but when it comes to waiting or creating things over time, individuals become more and more demanding and irrational. It can be about a kid pushing for a new toy, a new graduate, or an employee expecting the position of CEO to come simply by asking, whether it is simply a wish salary and work to simply come to them.

The good part I mentioned is that those who realize things take time have the persistence and commitment needed to get those things that others simply demand.

2. **Be Humble:** Humility in your behaviors helps to guarantee that you do not place your own opinions and worth above that of others.

   It is to ensure that you see yourself and others equally, and this will make certain scenarios and choices even more rational.

   Knowing that you are adequate as you are and that others are equally important will allow you to take everyone into account in conversations, choices, and life. Being humble is indeed a wonderful way to be more realistic.

3. **Ask for Support:** Many people want to feel that they can do it on their own and that they do not need assistance, and yet they can also see when someone else is hurting and not looking for help? It is peculiar that we let this ego keep us from just stopping and asking for help.

   However, when you do, particularly when others can already see it, you accept the need, and asking for support makes you appear honest and reasonable to see it for yourself.

   You lose the illusion people have and your reality of being able to do it on your own as you put on a façade that you can do it all yourself.

This generally leaves some damages or detrimental effects that you have never expected.

4. **Maintaining Focus:** The issue is not lack of time.

   The issue is the lack of direction. We all have the same 24-hour long days. We have multiple options when it comes to concentrating and focusing on what we expend our conscious time on. Have a look at our daily lives as an example.

   We have many choices, from the grocery store to the car selling outlets, that distract us from our attention. I will be the first to confess that 99% of the time, I get overwhelmed when I go to the grocery store for one thing and come home with much more than what I expected.

   Achievement is no different, we have priorities set, but we make decisions to invest time in less meaningful things, aspects that do not stress us or place us under pressure.

You can think in terms of either/or any moment you lose your focus:

- I can either write a few pages now, or I will have to wake up tomorrow with zero improvements in my novel.
- I can either work out right now, or I can continue in this body that I am so disappointed with.
- I can clean this house now, or I have decided to spend another day in a dirty, filthy house.
- Either I am starting my work hunt now, or I recognize that it is an extra week or even a month that I am going to be trapped in this job, I hate.

These were the six basic aspects you can adopt to develop a self-loving personality.

Chapter 2

How to Become More Seductive by Loving Yourself More

All of these factors combined make up what I believe to be self-love and if you want to learn to love yourself, you will need to learn and develop each of these components to healthy levels.

Since my aim in this book is to try to teach you how to love yourself correctly, I want you to understand what you need to have to be able to completely love yourself.

Self-Esteem

In the simplest of terms, self-esteem is generally what you think of yourself. It can be said that confident people have a high degree of self-esteem while those lacking in confidence have low self-esteem.

It usually develops through a combination of upbringing and personal experiences that shapes the way we view ourselves.

Most kids who grow up with loving parents initially develop a high level of self-esteem because parents would always tend to complement their child regardless of their actual abilities.

It is the same with society in general. Normal adults always praise children and are generally encouraging. No reasonable person would think to give a child negative criticism.

As a result, we as children have a high level of self-esteem because most of the feedback, we get is positive and adults try to be as kind to us as they can. As we grow up, the feedback we are given becomes more honest and our view of ourselves starts to shift into a more realistic one.

Self-Esteem is dynamic. It changes depending on a person's status and perception of themselves. During times of failure, self-esteem normally goes down because we generally also receive negative feedback while in periods of success, self-esteem goes up because the feedback we get is also positive. It is your evaluation of yourself, based on the feedback you get.

It is not always grounded in reality, and it can be subject to changes in a person's condition or social environment.

It is also a result of the accumulation of the experiences and affirmations that we have had since childhood which builds an image in our minds about who and what we are and where we ideally should stand in the social order.

Self-Confidence

Self-confidence generally refers to your faith in your abilities.

It develops from awareness or at least a perception of what you are capable of. For example, if you believe that you are terrible at math, then your confidence in tackling mathematical problems will naturally below.

If you think that you are a terrible dancer, then you would tend to avoid dancing-related activities.

Like I said earlier, it is about your faith in your abilities and is not always tied to reality. You can be confident about your singing abilities because you believe that you have a golden voice while in reality other people who hear you sing think the opposite.

Because of your misguided confidence in your singing abilities, you might be inclined to actively promote yourself as a singer regardless of what your actual voice quality is.

If you ever watch talent shows on TV, you will see a lot of people who have a high level of confidence in their abilities.

They view themselves as extremely talented and try to impress the judges and audience only to be disappointed when they do not win or even get angry if they receive fair criticism from the judges.

It is because self-confidence does not necessarily reflect your actual abilities but instead reflects what you think of your abilities. It is similar to self-esteem in that it usually comes from your upbringing and personal experiences, but it differs from it by being more specific.

You usually develop your confidence in particular abilities because of the feedback you have received whenever you display these abilities.

When I was little, I used to like singing in public. I used to sing at school presentations and I thought I had a great voice because my parents would always compliment me whenever I sang. During school presentations, the audience would clap after I sing and of course they did, what kind of adult would tell a child that their voice was terrible? This made me confident about my singing abilities.

When I grew up and started hanging out with people other than my parents, I started getting feedback that was not always positive whenever I sing.

Unfortunately, people become more honest in their feedback when you are no longer a child, so I lost confidence in my singing. While I still love to sing, I am no longer that confident that I would never sing on stage with an audience unless I was forced to do it.

Self-Acceptance

Self-Acceptance, on the other hand, is when you learn to accept yourself for what you are. It is when you forgive yourself for all your faults and failures.

It is when you appreciate your individuality regardless of how others perceive you.

It is close to self-love as having self-acceptance means recognizing your flaws and knowing all your negative traits but still appreciate yourself.

Unlike self-esteem and self-confidence which are generally affected by other people's feedback, self-acceptance is something you attain despite the feedback you get.

It is internal and more of a conscious choice rather than something that easily changes depending on what other people think.

When you learn to accept yourself, you do not judge yourself, and you do not compare yourself to others. It is being aware that you have specific weaknesses, but you do not let the awareness of these weaknesses bring down your opinion of yourself.

It is accepting your limitations as a human being. It is recognizing that you are not perfect, you make mistakes and you are not good at everything but still be okay with it. In other words, it is being contented with yourself.

Self-Awareness

Self-awareness is similar to self-acceptance in the sense that it is the acknowledgment of your traits.

It is about recognizing the changes in your emotions as they happen and exerting a degree of control of your actions following these emotional changes. It is understanding how these emotions affect your thought processes and knowing how you act in response to these emotions.

Having self-awareness is also similar to self-acceptance in that it is also about having an accurate assessment of your weaknesses and limitations, but unlike self-acceptance, it is more about knowing how these weaknesses and limitations affect the world around you. It is about knowing how to control your behavior despite your emotions instead of letting your emotions control how you behave.

It is like the idea of professionalism. You act according to how you are supposed to get the job done correctly, regardless of how you feel about your boss or your coworkers.

You treat your boss and your coworkers with respect despite feeling intense dislike for them because you understand that you need to cooperate with them to get the job done.

Having self-awareness means understanding that your emotional state can affect your performance and behavior.

It is knowing how to interact with your environment and other people in a morally acceptable manner despite your emotional state. Having self-awareness means that you know how to control yourself.

Self-Respect

In simple terms, having self-respect means having pride in yourself and as a result, you behave in such a way that upholds your sense of honor and dignity.

It is sometimes easy to confuse having a high degree of self-esteem or confidence with a high level of self-respect, but unlike self-esteem, having self-respect does not mean simply having a high opinion of yourself.

It is knowing what you are worth. It is having reasonable standards for yourself and behaving according to those standards. You do not settle for less because you know how much your worth and you do not hesitate to ask for what you deserve.

You are probably familiar with the phrase "Don't sink to their level" right? Having self-respect means exactly that. It means not compromising your standards for anyone, even if they do not have any standards. It is about valuing yourself and because you value yourself, you do not let other people treat you any less no matter who they are.

Having self-respect also means that you have integrity. Your standards apply regardless of the situation.

You do not bend your own rules or lower your standards just because it is easier to do so in certain situations.

If you have self-respect, you do not feel the need to beg for anyone's approval because for you, just knowing your worth is all the approval you need.

Self-respect combines the elements of self-esteem, self-acceptance, and self-awareness in that you have a reasonable opinion of yourself, you are aware of your weaknesses and limitations, and you keep your actions within an acceptable moral standard.

It means knowing who and what you are and taking responsibility for your actions. It means that you feel worthy of being loved and accepted by others. It is acting with honor and dignity because you know that you deserve to be treated with respect.

It also means knowing how to properly ask for what you deserve and standing up for yourself if you are not treated with respect.

You do not allow other people to give you less than what you ask for and you do not let other people disrespect you.

As a result, having self-respect means you also treat others with the same level of respect because you know that treating other people poorly demeans you.

Having self-respect also tends to make other people treat you with respect because they see that you have standards and that you behave according to your standards.

Personal Empowerment

Personal empowerment is positively taking control of your life.

It is taking all the above factors to determine your worth and then using everything you know about yourself to set realistic goals and using your abilities to achieve them.

It is knowing your weaknesses and aiming to improve on them, and it is knowing your strengths and using them to advance yourself.

Having personal empowerment means knowing how to take control of your circumstances to achieve your personal goals.

It is also about understanding your strengths and weaknesses well, making you better equipped in dealing with any problems that you encounter. You know how to recognize opportunities and know how to take advantage of them appropriately to succeed.

It does not simply mean having the power to make things happen. It also means knowing how to set realistic goals and having the freedom and the ability to make conscious decisions and taking the appropriate actions to achieve these goals.

Chapter 3

Building and Mastering Emotions

Being aware of our emotions also means knowing that our emotions can drive our behavior and impact those around us, either positively or negatively. It also means we can manage these emotions, that of our own and that of others, especially at pressuring and stressful times.

The Five Categories of Emotional Intelligence (EQ)

When it comes to Emotional Intelligence, five categories becomes a focus.

1.   Self-awareness.

Having self-awareness means having the ability to recognize an emotion as and when it occurs and it is the key to your EQ.

To develop self-awareness, a person needs to tune into their true feelings, evaluating them, and subsequently managing them. In self-awareness, the important elements are:

- Recognizing our own emotions and their effects
- Having a level of confidence and sureness of your capabilities and your self-worth

2.   Self-regulation.

When we experience emotions, we often have little control over our actions when we first feel these emotions. One thing we can control however is how long these emotions last.

To control how long certain emotions last, especially negative ones, certain methods are used to lessen the effects of these emotions such as anxiety, anger, and even depression. These methods include reinventing a scenario in a much positive manner such as through taking a long walk, saying a prayer, and even meditating.

Self-regulation includes:

- Innovation means open to new ideas
- Adaptability to handle change and be flexible
- Trustworthiness referring to the ability to keep to standards of integrity and honesty
- Taking responsibility, the conscientiousness of our actions
- Self-control to prevent disruptive impulses

3. Motivation

Having motivation is what keeps us going to accomplish our tasks and goals and to maintain an air of positivity.

With practice and with effort, we can all program our minds to be more positive although as human beings, it is also good to be negative at times. This does not mean having negative thoughts are bad, but these thoughts need to be kept in check as they cause more harm than good.

Whenever you feel like you have negative feelings, you can also reprogram them to be more positive or at least to pick out the positive aspects of the situation, the silver lining which will help you be more focused on solving the problem.

Motivation is made up of:

- Having the sense of achievement drive, to constantly strive to improve and meet a level of excellence.
- Committing to align your individual, group, or organizational goals
- Having the initiative to act on available opportunities
- Having the optimism to pursue your goals persistently and objectively, despite the setbacks and obstacles.

4. Empathy

Empathy is the ability to recognize how people would feel towards a certain scenario, thing, or person. Having this ability is crucial to success both in a career as with life. The more you can decipher the feelings of people, the better you can manage the thoughts and approaches you send them. Empathetic people are excellent at:

- Recognizing, anticipating, and meeting a person's needs
- Developing the needs of other people and bolstering their abilities
- Taking advantage of diversity by cultivating opportunities among different people
- Developing political awareness by understanding the current emotional state of people and fostering powerful relationships
- Focusing on identifying feelings and wants of other people

5. Social skills.

Developing good interpersonal skills is imperative as well if you want a successful life and a successful career. In our world today when plenty of things are digitized, social skills seem to be an afterthought.

People skills are more relevant and sought-after than before especially since now you also need a high EQ to understand, negotiate and empathize with others especially if you deal and interact with different people daily. Among the most useful skills are:

- Influence to effectively wield persuasive tactics

- Communication to send our clear and concise messages
- Leadership to inspire and guide people and groups.
- Change catalyst in kick-starting and managing change
- Managing conflicting situations which include the ability to negotiate, understand and resolve disagreements
- To bond and nurture meaningful and instrumental relationships
- Teamwork, cooperation, and collaboration in meeting shared goals
- Creating a synergetic group to work towards collective goals.

Creating a Balance with Emotional Awareness

As a human being, emotions and feelings make up every aspect of our existence. Managing them and keeping them balanced will help us reach our maximum potential in life, at work, and especially in our relationships.

As we know by now, having a good emotional balance leads us towards better physical and mental health, making life happier.

When our emotional well-being is disrupted, this will result in the opposite. Our physical health will decline, we will start having digestive problems, lack of energy, and sleep issues.

People with emotional distress often exhibit low self-esteem, they are self-critical and pessimistic. They always need to assert themselves through their behavior. They are overly worried, get afraid very fast, and are focused on the past.

The connection between our Thoughts and Feelings

Thoughts determine our feelings and they are nothing more than firing the neurons in our body. Our thoughts also generate feelings, making our body release additive natural substances such as cortisol and adrenaline.

The connection between the body and the mind is extremely vivid and strong, strong enough that the mental and physical state sends positive and negative vibes both ways.

The feelings we experience depends on our thought, combined with our attitudes and actions.

Emotions are part of our daily life and we experience this every day. What we want is to strike a balance in our emotions, thoughts, and feelings to ensure that they do not adversely affect our daily tasks and cause us stress.

Creating Emotional Balance

So how we do create emotional balance? Emotional balance is the ability to maintain equilibrium and flexibility between the mind and body when we are faced with changes or challenges.

Here are some ways that you can create emotional balance:

1. Accept your emotions

Many of our mental, emotional and physical problems stem from our inability to express ourselves emotionally.

When we experience an emotionally distraught, we smother it in the comforts of eating, sleeping, sweating it out, sucking it up, it is swept under a rug, we bury it, project it elsewhere, meditate even all in the hopes of suppressing our emotions instead of dealing with it by accepting that this is what we are going through right not. The key here is to allow ourselves unconditional permission to feel- to cry when we want to, to feel anger when we are angry, sadness when we grief and so on. Let your guard down either when you are alone or with someone you trust and just focus on the feeling and situation.

Experience and immerse yourself in this feeling so you can comprehend better why it hurts and what you will be doing to remedy the situation once you've accepted and acknowledged these feelings.

2. Express yourself

Expressing yourself is important. There are many ways to express oneself and usually when we experience a feeling, we react by crying, shouting, throwing things.

But to identify with ourselves and be able to manage our emotions properly, we can also express ourselves in more positive ways. Some people like reading as it provides an escape into a different world.

Some people express themselves through art or music.

Whatever it is that you do, make sure you stay connected to discover more about yourself, your identity, and also the person you want to become.

3. Don't shove your feelings

Sometimes, it is easy to shove our feelings and not think about them, especially painful and scary memories.

But as we all know, stuffing your memories and feelings will only make things worse for you.

While it is hard to address your fears and sadness, rage and anger, once you dive into it, you will find that it will become easier to face your fears, and eventually, the choppy waters will become calmer. Be accepting your past and dealing with it in a more emotional state, you ultimately will lead a harmonious life. Always allow yourself to feel because your reactions to these different feelings would be in a more stable way rather than an overreaction.

4. See the world in a positive light

It is easier said than done, we know. In a world full of hatred, sadness, grief, war, crime, unfairness - it is a threat to our emotional health.

You tend to develop low self-esteem and start asking yourself if you are worth it if you can get through it if you are doing things right and all this thinking steers you towards making more mistakes and missteps.

Rather than having emotional self-doubt, take action to develop a prerogative of seeing the world in a more positive light.

Do not feel responsible for the bad things that happen which are not caused by you is a good start. Have compassion in yourself and practice mindfulness and accept that occasional lapses and failures are just part of being human.

5. Get a grip on your mind

The way we think causes us emotional distress- this probably is not news to you. We all have this tendency into overthinking and these thoughts that do not serve you or give you any positivity is just setting you up for emotional distress. So, get a grip on your mind- do not let it wander too much especially when you start overthinking.

6. Practice Yoga and Mindfulness

Doing yoga daily does help in your mental health- it helps by increasing your confidence in your abilities and it also helps you make better definitive decisions. You also learn to not be so self-criticizing. Yoga, practiced daily can help get rid of negative energy within you and help you work your way towards mental clarity and vital energy. Not only that, the breathing that is practiced in yoga helps you relax better, make you calmer especially if your mind is racing and it also helps you to refine your feelings.

Breathing correctly helps you get rid of stress and anxiety as well.

Chapter 4

Embrace the Vulnerability of Self-Care

Have you ever been the odd one out in an argument? Imagine you are with a group of friends, and the group begins gossiping about a friend that isn't present. It makes you uncomfortable, but you feel self-conscious about speaking up.

It's so much easier just to stay quiet, nod, and laugh along with your friends. In your head, you debate whether to stick up for your friend, voice your discomfort, and risk being shamed by the group. In this situation, being accepted socially comes at odds with acting in alignment with your values.

This is a common dilemma in life, so use the example scenario as an opportunity to dig deeper.

Is the short-term gratification of social acceptance worth the long-term feeling of disappointment of not sticking up for yourself and your friend?

Do you see how taking risks to honor your values may be the more self-loving option in the long-run?

Do you think acting in alignment with your values, while vulnerable and sometimes scary, would lead to more self-love in the long-run?

Choosing to stand up for our values will always be a vulnerable endeavor. Building a self-love practice is also a vulnerable endeavor. Both of these acts force us to forgo instant gratification and take a look at what feels true to us.

We have to be okay with feeling soft, vulnerable, and open to the judgment of others.

We have to be okay with going against the grain, slowing down, admitting we have reached our limits or admitting we need help.

The vulnerability of taking care of ourselves, or even admitting that we need care in the first place, maybe why some avoid this topic. However, when we embrace self-care and vulnerability, they make our self-love practices so much richer.

Getting Comfortable with Vulnerability

Self-love is vulnerable because sometimes, the people around you don't want you to put yourself first. If you're used to prioritizing the desires of others before your own, choosing to honor yourself might disrupt old relationship dynamics.

At this stage, you need to be ready for two things to happen:

1. You need to be ready to be challenged for your decision to choose yourself.
2. You need to be ready to stick with the decision, even if it causes a disruption or conflict.

Though sometimes this can cause disruption, usually, we magnify the impact in our minds. No, choosing yourself doesn't mean deliberately hurting the people around you.

It means having the courage to think about what you want and honor yourself by making the desire known.

This can play out in even the simplest of scenarios. Imagine you are making dinner plans with a group of coworkers.

The group is trying to decide between burgers, tacos, or sushi.

You've been wanting to try the sushi place for months, and don't care for the other two options. It would be so simple to voice this, but you don't want to sway the group, and you know you can find something on any menu.

We tend to think people prefer easygoing friends, but in this case, most people would prefer to know your preference.

This example may seem silly, but even the small decisions in our lives add up.

Each time you take the risk of voicing your preference, no matter how simple, you get to know yourself a bit better. You tell yourself that your preferences matter.

You take a bit of power back in your life, and your inner self feels the love in these gestures.

Here are a few more examples of small gestures that can help you practice being vulnerable and voicing your truth:

- Telling your partner, you'd like to go on a date this week
- Asking to take a short break to drink some water during a meeting
- Telling your family, you need half an hour of alone time in the evenings
- Leaving a party when you are ready to go, even if you're the first one to leave
- Telling your friends that you would prefer not to participate in gossip
- Asking for help with a household chore
- Asking a friend for advice
- Asking to sit outside if the noise in the restaurant is bothering you

As you can see, there are quite a few opportunities throughout the day for you to stick up for yourself. Sometimes the small desires we have can feel so meaningless that we don't even give them a second thought.

If you feel like you don't even know your preferences sometimes, tuning into these small moments can help you strengthen that inner knowledge.

Getting comfortable with vulnerability will help you get to know and learn to trust yourself.

Each time you honor your preferences, you strengthen the message of self-love that you are sending to your inner self.

The Vulnerability of Self-Care

Strengthening your ability to be vulnerable is a key ingredient for consistent self-care. Self-care is taking deliberate action to nurture your inner self.

If you have been hard on yourself in the past, it can also be vulnerable for your inner self to acknowledge and accept new gestures of self-love.

Just like a child, your inner self may be skeptical of something they haven't yet learned to trust. If you feel resistant to developing a self-love practice, this could be why.

You may find that you are afraid to trust yourself. Maybe trying something new led you to criticize yourself harshly in the past.

It takes time, patience, and consistency to repair this relationship with yourself, but I think if you've read this far, you know this endeavor is worthwhile.

To be vulnerable, we need to feel safe to be our authentic selves. On the path to self-love, this means learning to feel at home in our skin. Maybe your body and mind have not felt like the safest places to be in the past.

Maybe you are hard on yourself. Maybe you endure mental or physical stress to punish yourself for not being good enough.

Maybe you suppress certain emotions or try to numb any pain you feel. These are all ways we can teach ourselves that our bodies and minds are not safe places.

Once we learn this, we accept it as a fact. It becomes subconscious, and we don't give it much thought.

It takes some undoing and relearning to get to a place where we feel safe in our bodies and minds again.

Here are a few examples of ways you can begin to feel more comfortable and safer within your body and mind:

Action:	The message this sends to your inner self:
Do some stretches before bed.	I love my body and believe that it deserves to feel relaxed and calm.
Journal some positive thoughts about yourself.	I may not be perfect, but I love myself anyway. I deserve a mind that loves me rather than punishes me.
Take some time to enjoy a nice drink with no screens or distractions.	I deserve to create a calming, restorative space to relax my body and mind.
Plan a morning routine that you are excited to wake up for.	My needs are unique to me. They are worth learning and honoring. I am willing to do what it takes to trust myself again.

For some people, it can be challenging to see the point in forming new habits, putting in a bit of extra effort, and sticking with something you may feel you don't have time for. Trust me, I get it. But these tiny actions are where big change can happen.

Learn to see your body and mind as your home. Build the home up with kind thoughts, loving care, and calming routines.

Put your preferences at the forefront, and show yourself that this is the new way the house is run.

Slowly, you'll begin to feel safe opening up and living fully within your own space.

Chapter 5

How To Overcome Self Doubt?

Discovering how to resolve self-doubt and fear is one of life's most difficult challenges. Just how great our quality is depending a lot on how much self-confidence we have because anxiety is an uncommon sort of internal torment that can quickly slip into.

So how do you resolve the fears, difficulties, and anxieties that overtake your thoughts? To order to achieve better, what can you do to trust yourself? How can you resolve the self-doubt that stops you from succeeding?

Self-doubt is a position where we were both but each one of us struggles with it differently. Doubt and anxiety are difficult to control and are usually deep in our heads. An error, a mistake, or even a minor loss, lets you doubt and challenge your ability.

Next thing you know, there's a lack of trust.

Once you start a business or have a theory, self-doubt always crawls in as you continue to equate yourself to those who have been good before you and are overwhelmed by the thought of how much effort you have to put in.

You're also starting to think at that stage that there's no chance you can ever make it as successful people do.

But success is the courage to move in the direction of your dreams and on the path your heart takes you. It doesn't matter if you don't do it just like those before you do.

You should understand that self-doubt is not a rational behavior and that you can go beyond it.

"Self-doubt ruins more illusions than ever do defeat."-Suzy Kassem None of us will ever be completely free from doubts. Everybody, no matter how successful, always struggle with it. But if you let it take hold, self-doubt can become a self-fulfilling prophecy. You may have tried to achieve an objective in the past and decided to give up when you met an obstacle that seemed difficult, but you shouldn't give up.

It's the way life is! Goals get you out of the comfort zone, put you into new territory, and with your doubts and fears, take you head-on.

The question here is not how to overcome self-doubt and anxiety, but how to make constructive decisions that improve your self-confidence while there are uncertainties.

Due to self-doubt, insecurity, loss of faith, or terror, too many people give up on their aspirations.

Moving past self-doubt and fear

Essentially all successful people have admitted that every single day they have to battle self-doubt.

Doubt is so harmful that countless people are discouraged from doing beautiful things. Yet anxiety is not who you are at all, but rather an event you're passing through.

It doesn't make them go away if you're trying to avoid uncertainty and anxiety. It doesn't make it any less unpleasant if you neglect certain thoughts, and if you look the other way, it doesn't help them disappear into thin air.

Now take a deep breath. Then know that you still need to take action, even if you have questions or a deep fear hits you. Avoid crippling self-doubt and take the necessary steps to achieve your goals.

Overcoming Self-Doubt

It is always easier to say than done to remove doubts on the spot. But below are ways to start conquering self-doubt to accomplish the goals you have wanted.

Remove Wrong Words

You must remove from your vocabulary any words that seem wrong. The expressions, sentences, and verbs that you use to refer to yourself can shake off your confidence. Often these wrong words are untrue.

Instead, delete or skip terms like "never," "still," "can't," "no one," "when," and "will." Then you'll see that the frame of mind or self-doubt can change for the better.

Recognize Self-Doubt

It is necessary to identify suspicions that are not an easy task. To create a business, a website, or even an app, you might have a great idea. Yet if you think you can't just quit your job to move into something else, you could shrug it off.

You've got to pay for a home and a mortgage. And who is going to pay for the bills?

There are, of course, still threats. But if you don't feel you can be good, you're not going to guess anything. And, if you force a thought away next time, wonder seriously if it's the self-doubt and truth that sneaked in.

Get Daily Dose of Inspiration

Subscribe to podcasts, watch videos, read books, or watch inspiring films. It can allow you to resolve whatever doubts and fears you may have. You may also feel empowered to act.

You can also find some great conversation leaders and advisors. When you lack self-confidence, turn to these men.

Also popular was Overcome Self-Doubt Dumber men. You have to remember that you are an intelligent and capable person.

The explanation is that in this universe there are individuals who have done greater things with less expertise, resources, incentives, and experience than you have.

You have to note that you've been effective for others with less benefit than you.

It is difficult or even futile to handle some desire or vision of yours. The hurdle you have to conquer most of the time is self-doubt.

Reflect on previous achievements

Are you focused on the bad like the mistakes you have encountered when you wake up or during the day? Or on the better like the wins, you've won?

Recent studies have shown that how you recall the history determines what you feel of yourself now.

Your feelings on yourself have a huge impact on any future actions you take and how well they work out for you.

Check for reviews

The quest for input from others is also great. Having a conversation about your skills and abilities with those who help you and are around you can stop self-doubt right on the spot.

However, above all, seeking input can make you see both the positive and negative aspects of your skills. As a consequence, some of the necessary skills can be improved.

Be mindful of Doubt from Others

Self-doubt is already difficult to deal with, but other people's suspicions are only frustrating.

Once you know that you are starting to gain more self-confidence and ability, you may find other people around you, even nearer than you expect, who are focusing their self-doubt on you. They're certainly going to try to shoot down your dreams or even find reasons why you shouldn't pursue them.

But let me still tell you to act on your ideas.

Celebrate Small Wins

This absorbs you whenever you're caught in the pit of self-doubt. Even if it's not true in fact, you could make it accurate and make it a big deal in your head.

To sink to that point, it took you a series of small acts.

Okay, to get out, it will also take small yet necessary moves. This motivates you when you enjoy small wins because you see progress being made and you create momentum that easily adds up.

More Strategies to Conquer Self Doubt

- Self-doubt is difficult to conquer, but almost anyone with the will can do it.
- Brainstorm any event, process, or initiative you feel will help you achieve success.
- Remember all the things you know to do and abilities you can learn quickly.
- Start learning and bringing these different skills and abilities into action.
- Believe that you can do better to do more.
- Draw the inspiration well from the left, and focus on acts that deliver results.
- Stay away from self-doubt by taking small steps contributing to progress and working on the next.

- Activate the internal genius and disregard self-doubt or criticism.

Even when other people tell you that you can't do it, or that it's an impossible dream, or that it's impractical, it's not easy to get going and give up, but use their skepticism as a reason to prove them wrong.

A symptom of self-doubt is when you let other people's opinions and self-doubt affect you on your vision and concept to take action. You have to carefully pick your thoughts because they become your impulses which determine your actions in effect.

Undoubtedly, there will be questions in your heart. Therefore, you have to choose not to accept the feelings that offer you such suspicions to overcome self-doubt.

Uncertainties, worries, and suspicions are always going to be part of your life, but you are the one who chooses to believe them or not.

This presumption of achievement is important because if you allow self-doubt (the fear of failure) to enter, you can erode the prospects of positive practice. The lack of action, not, in general, any failures, is what keeps you from moving towards your objectives.

Life is too short to allow that to happen, so let's look at why people are struggling with self-doubt and some fast actions you should take in the next ten minutes to make sure you don't get out of the stuff you want to do.

Where does self-doubt come from?

Well, this comes through two types of pessimistic anticipation-first, the assumption that it might not be possible to achieve the target itself, and second, the perception that even if the goal is possible, it will likely not be achievable for you.

Everyone daily thinks like these at some level. Let's concentrate on how to defuse their power to create self-doubt in the first place, an active two-step method.

Step 1

Note that it is not difficult for someone to achieve the goal itself.

There's a lot of silent "self-talk" going on every day in your mind. There's a part of you staring at the limitless possibilities before you... And then there's the other part of you that advises you to be "fair," the bar is set so low, the goal is simply not achievable.

Today, many people face the problem of not even realizing that this discussion is taking place. They're likely to just go through the motions and ponder why they're motivated to take initiative occasionally, and sometimes they're not.

That may describe you (and I know it's been defining me many times in my life, so I'm speaking here from personal experience).

Nonetheless, the way to avoid self-doubt is to take full and absolute care of that interaction. To learn to listen carefully to the value of the discussion that takes place in your mind and to take command when it doesn't go the way it needs to be.

The way to start doing this is by trying to look objectively at the case-that is, by keeping oneself out of the equation.

Instead of worrying about what you can and can't do, look at the target and note that a human being can't achieve it. It could certainly be done by somebody on Earth (or has already achieved this).

Rehearse a phrase that you can use to break the habit of thought which stops you from being 100% sure that you can achieve your goal is the way to do this job. Let's say your goal in the next 12 months is to become fully financially independent.

While this may appear to many to be a daunting task, it is certainly not impossible. People are doing this all the time.

So maybe your answer would be something like this: "Within 12 months or less, it's not difficult to become financially independent. It's been achieved over and over again." Well, why do I choose to say "It's not unlikely..." rather than the more optimistic "It's feasible..." sound? The response is because I don't want to give you a chance to justify using the term "but."

You know, they always feel "Yes, it's conceivable, however." If you reply "It's not unlikely..." you actively resist the opportunity to come up with a good argument to challenge the capacity to do it.

You are forced to admit that there is no immovable, unstoppable force that stops you from achieving your goal at all times. Your focus is on the fact that at any given time the potential exists, no matter how you "feel" about it.

Do not make the mistake of taking this step as a matter of course, because it is essential. The universal assumptions that you have about life-what are likely and what is not-drive your acts on a day-to-day basis.

We control where you can go, like the strings of a puppet. So, you must be careful to get them right and never lose sight of the fact that you can do just about anything.

Sidebar: This is not positive thinking I'm writing about here just to clarify things. I don't say you're going to succeed because you're saying "I think I can." It's realistic thinking that I'm talking about-focusing on facts, not emotions.

Looking critically at stuff. Taking personal anxiety out of the equation and realizing your ability as an individual being-not as the array of skills and experiences you label "you."

To sum up this first step, you need to have a strong statement (or series of them) that you can concentrate on having your head firmly rooted in the fact-the reality that your objective is by no means impossible.

It may be challenging, and it may demand more of yourself than you have ever provided, but it is not impossible. In reality, it is impossible with the right commitment and strategies.

You are ready to move on to the next stage once you have presented the target logically in your head this way, and you are convinced that your aim is not impossible to achieve.

Step 2

Note that you cannot achieve the goal itself - particularly -.

A lot of people get into trouble here. We claim, "Yes, it's conceivable, but not for me."

That's where we step into the magical world of explanations, where every challenge seems to be eternal and far too difficult to overcome. To change the situation, we see ourselves as relatively powerless.

However, in reality, we have a huge amount of power. If we dwell on our shortcomings, whether it's energy, cash, ability, whatever that's when we turn over that control to the side of us thinking "you really can't do it."

Its part of us concentrating on what we can't do has a long list of all the excuses why we're not up to the task, and it's pretty hard to refute it. You realize I'm thinking about the sound.

So, the secret of it all is turning the tables around and making a clear list of all the benefits you should do it - and why you're just the one to do it, in general.

It's not the same as reading a review. You think long and hard about how you're going to verbalize why you're more than qualified to do the job when you want to apply for a new position.

You mention your qualifications, training, wealth, and above all, your accomplishments and achievements.

If you give that to a hiring manager, the hope is that they will look at it and say, "Oh, this guy is just the one to get the job done." In creating a resume for yourself, you will build the same feeling of confidence. You have to put aside some time and do some hard thinking to do this and do it correctly. You need to brag about yourself and note all the knowledge you've taken for granted.

You have all the tools you can manage. You have all the experience from which you can benefit.

There's so much more to it than you know right now because you've let your ambitions obstacles transform your attention to your failures and weaknesses. But it is time to strike hard now.

Now you've got to do that

If you want to conquer self-doubt permanently, this is the important part. You need to take this advice and put it into action. Read this post and do the job, and you will immediately begin to see progress.

And if you don't feel like doing it now, and think to yourself, "That may be feasible to you, but it's not for me," bookmark this post and read it every day. Ultimately, you're going to get fed up with the reasons and decide to act.

Abraham Maslow claims that raising your self-esteem is centered on the essence of psychological health, and it is achievable only when the basic heart of the individual is genuinely understood, loved, and respected by others and by himself or herself. Jack

Canfield says: "Self-esteem is focused on feeling lovable and worthy."

Self-esteem is interrelated with self-image. The word self-image is used to define the self-image of a person's mind. Image of yourself leads to self-esteem.

We develop mental representations of ourselves during early childhood: what we are, what we are good at, what we feel, and what our strengths and weaknesses might be. The memories and the relationships with other individuals will reinforce these mental images within us. Such mental self-images can grow our self-esteem notion over time. Self-esteem is about feelings we develop as a result of external factors within ourselves.

Self-esteem is about how much other people accept, love, and appreciate us, and how much we recognize, support, and praise ourselves. Their self-esteem is formed by the synthesis of these two variables.

Generally, in terms of how we view ourselves and our attributes, self-esteem is described. According to Stanley Coppersmith, a leading scholar in the area, it is "a personal judgment of worthiness that is reflected in the individual's attitudes toward himself." Good self-esteem implies that we have enough self-confidence not to need the validation of others.

Chapter 6

Confidence and Self-motivation

How do you perceive yourself? Do you think you are strong?

Can you manage anything that happens in the day or weeks ahead? Do you break down when things get a little tough? Do you project your feelings or actions onto others? Do you feel you are hiding your inability?

The above questions relate to confidence and how you perceive yourself. Some people keep going, doing, and never seem to falter.

Others talk down about themselves, yet still, accomplish plenty. Some individuals will project their feelings and it is the appearance of being "perfect" that motivates them, while ultimately, they lack confidence.

Before you can begin to gain self-motivation and improve your confidence, you need to understand who you are and why you should be working on these two concepts.

Why Learn to Motivate Yourself

We all have dreams. When in depression, we sometimes forget about those dreams and believe we cannot accomplish them at all. We feel we are spinning our wheels, struggling, and perhaps it is someone else's fault rather than our own.

Have you had a struggle such as this? Are you in one now?

Depression is just one effect that may cause a lack of self-motivation and confidence. For other individuals, their childhood path never gave them the desire to be motivated.

Perhaps you always had someone to depend on, to motivate you to do things, and that has continued into adulthood.

Consider for a moment that path of the woman in the '50s.

Many women were brought up with minimal schooling, told they would not need college, but rather an etiquette school to learn how to be wives, mothers, and the home support for their working husbands.

The idea that some would go to college existed, but most often these were ladies' colleges offering courses in art or teaching, and not areas like science and engineering.

The motivation was always about their husband and family. In the same vein, it also created numerous struggles and unhappy moments.

The motivation for these women was based on their upbringing and what they were told they could or could not achieve.

Think about how you would feel if your parents told you college was out of the question and all you could do was go to a trade school, marry, and raise children.

How would you react? Perhaps, you have been told this as it does still happen today.

You might have the thoughts that you want to change this outlook, you want your kids to have more opportunities, and later in life, you finally decide to do something to make changes.

It is not only your obligation to ensure the female gender is regarded with equality but something you should desire in your heart.

We can all have the family, happy marriage, and career we want, if we are motivated enough to get it.

If you do not want to feel stuck in the '50s with only a few choices and a path that ends in an unhappy marriage, then you must take control of your life and learn how you can motivate yourself.

Yes, upbringing is a part of it. We do learn from our parents, their perceptions, lessons, and thoughts, but as a human with free will, you truly have the choice to improve your life based on your dreams. It doesn't matter how long it takes you to realize these dreams, what matters is you are willing to try.

Plenty of things can get in the way from your upbringing to social perceptions, even your own biases. It is going to take stepping back and viewing your life, what you desire, and who you want to become before you will find motivation.

It may take all the above to discover "why" you should find self-motivation.

Exercise for the 'Why'

Why are some women more motivated than others?

Consider Oprah as an example. She has risen to new heights in stardom, with acting in movies, running her talk show, her TV channel, starting a magazine, and writing books.

What motivated her? Interviews she has done say she wanted to prove that as a woman of African American heritage, it was possible to be successful, to help other women realize their potential, and be an inspiration. She has certainly been all those things.

Why might a woman try to harm her family, even though she is divorced? What would keep motivating her to spend energy on negative and destructive pathways?

Money, hate, an inability to genuinely love herself? There are positive and negative reasons one might consider using self-motivation in life.

Before going into the exercise, it is helpful to point out that there is a difference between self-motivation for progress and positive feelings and the "negative" reasons you might motivate yourself into doing something.

It is time to discover "why" you want to find self-motivation:

- What are your dreams?
- Do your dreams feel achievable?
- How can you choose one dream and make it a reality?
- Are you unhappy with your choices in life?
- What can you do to alleviate the negative feelings and find positive emotions?

You do not have to have answers to every question right now. The idea is to discover who you are and why you have the dreams or goals that you keep dwelling on.

You sought out a guide for self-motivation because something was making you unhappy. You are trying to find a new way to approach life and reach the dreams you keep dwelling on.

The exercise is asking for you to take the first step and write the goals down. When you can visualize them on paper, they become more real.

It is also a way for you to examine the goals in full and decide what is achievable in your current situation and what may need to change.

Often the first step to finding more motivation or any at all is to address why you are unhappy and what you can do to ensure a more positive outlook. It takes time.

For now, the "why" of learning self-motivation techniques are the most important. As you move through the guide, you will be given more exercises and information to help you reach your goals.

How important is Motivation

Self-motivation provides us with the ability to protect our interests. Without the psychological process of motivation, by which we act, we would not reach our objectives or goals.

Using motivation allows us to put away our weaknesses and concentrate on the strengths.

Motivation is highly imperative to one's success. It offers:
- Commitment
- Personal Drive
- Optimism
- Initiative

Commitment comes into play when you have personal or career-related goals. Personal drive is all about the desire to meet goals, or even exceed your standards. Optimism helps you assess life without the negatives holding you back.

The initiative is the part of the motivation that helps you to be ready for any opportunity that might present itself.

Those who are self-motivated often have confidence, time management skills, and are organized.

When assessing your reasons for self-motivation, we discussed societal preconceptions and pressures, which are extrinsic factors.

To help others, to be productive in your career, even the feedback of others can be motivating for you.

The intrinsic factors are usually based on feelings, such as love or the desire to follow through. With "self" motivation being intrinsic you are more likely to perform an act for the satisfaction it provides versus extrinsic factors that demand satisfaction from others.

You can be motivated in different ways, using both intrinsic and extrinsic concepts. What becomes of a person who is not self-motivated or even motivated is - well - nothing?

They do not reach their goals, they spin their wheels in the same dead-end jobs, and never reach happiness.

Motivation is important for several reasons:
- To feel love for yourself, and to accept it from others.
- To be happy in your life, and the choices you make.
- To lead by example for new generations.
- To attain goals and dreams you have.
- To be able to take the initiative on projects and opportunities.
- To stick with something, you start and finish it to the end

Without motivation, nothing would be accomplished. We would not have reached the moon, households would not have personal computers, cars would not be a thing, and the list of inventions can go on.

No motivation equals a lack of safety, personal triumph, and health care when you think on a global scale.

You are ready to proceed in your education about how the brain works, and the concept of neuroplasticity, which will lead you to an understanding of how you can develop self-motivation no matter your age.

Chapter 7

The Signs That You Lack of Self-Love

1) You're Too Focused on Productivity and Feel Guilty About Taking a Break or Having Fun

Wanting to be more productive is a good thing. You want to be able to do more work and accomplish more of your tasks and goals that you set, however, if you're too into your work and don't think that you deserve a break or if having fun is no longer a part of your process, then perhaps it's time to take a step back and re-evaluate.

As they say, too much of a good thing can be bad, and taking a break and having fun is something that should be done on occasion.

It's okay to prioritize work and productivity especially when you have a deadline or a pile of work needing to be finished and when you're still okay with taking a break when you get tired or overwhelmed.

It's a problem when you start thinking that you don't deserve to take a break or when you take a break and have fun only to feel guilty about it later.

You keep pushing yourself to the limit and you feel that taking even a short break is a waste of your precious time.

You work yourself to death because you believe that taking time to have fun or spend time with your loved ones keeps you away from becoming successful.

Loving yourself means also making yourself happy and if you're not doing things that make you happy then it means you don't love yourself enough.

2) You Believe that You're Stuck with Current Situation and You No Longer Have Any Dreams and Aspirations

Have you completely given up on your dreams? Have you completely given up on making things better? Some people just develop so much self-doubt that they no longer believe that they can ever achieve anything meaningful.

Without having dreams of better things or aspiring to something greater than your current situation, you are completely wasting your potential.

It's one thing to feel contentment where you feel that you've already achieved everything you can, and it's another thing to feel that you can't achieve anything and completely give up on trying.

You probably still have dreams of a better life or improving your situation but you're no longer doing anything to reach those dreams or improve your situation because you've accepted that this is your lot in life.

You let this limiting belief take you over and your life has become stagnant.

You stop believing in your potential and you let yourself settle for mediocrity. You feel like it's futile to even try because you're sure that trying will only fail.

You hate your current situation but you're scared to make changes because you're afraid that you'll only make things worse.

3) You Keep Comparing Yourself to Others and are Extremely Self-Critical

Everyone is unique. Each of us has a unique set of circumstances, personalities, talents, and abilities.

Some people are simply better than others in some things and that's just a fact of life. It's okay to feel a little envious over what other people have that we don't and it's okay to have people whom we think are better than us.

It's also okay to be a little self-critical especially when we screw up and it's okay to be a little insecure about some small part of ourselves. That's just the way things are.

Sometimes we can't help but compare ourselves with other people. It's what makes the advertising industry lucrative.

We see a beautiful actress using an anti-aging cream and we want to look young and beautiful like this actress, so we buy the product.

Men want to look as big and strong as the athletes featured on supplement labels so they buy the supplements hoping to get the same results.

We naturally compare ourselves to other people, especially the ones who we think are doing better than us

The problem is when comparing yourself to someone else becomes excessive to the point of obsession and you can't seem to stop doing it.

It's a problem when you start seeing yourself as ultimately inferior to other people and you start punishing yourself for making small mistakes and when you feel like you're not as good as someone else.

You get frustrated and start loathing yourself for not having what other people have or not getting the same results as others. You blame yourself for everything that goes wrong even if it's something that's beyond your control.

You consider yourself a failure because you're not as successful as someone you know.

4) You Hate the Way You Look

Related to the previous entry, this is when you can't accept something about your physical attributes.

While feeling a little insecure about some part of your body and features is normal, it becomes a problem when you let the insecurity consume you and you become overly self-critical of your physical features and punish yourself.

This punishment can come in the form of giving up on trying to look good. You stop fixing your hair, you stop caring about what clothes to wear, you stop grooming yourself and you stop caring about eating healthy and getting regular exercise.

Sometimes the punishment takes on the exact opposite.

You become extremely obsessed with looking perfect that you spend all your money on fancy things, even going as far as getting plastic surgery because you want to look perfect.

Eventually, you develop a host of issues like eating disorders and body dysmorphia because you are obsessed with your physical appearance. No amount of makeup, clothes, or body modifications is enough to make you feel beautiful.

You crave for perfection that you will never realistically achieve and you go to extraordinary lengths, even taking huge risks just to look perfect.

5) You Have Extremely High-Risk Tendencies

It's okay to take occasional, calculated risks if you stand to gain something. However, it's different when you are actively making choices that you already know you'll regret later or taking an unnecessarily high amount of risk.

It's an even more dangerous sign when you deliberately put yourself in harm's way for cheap thrills.

This reminds me of a good friend back in college who had gambling problems and a generally high-risk tendency.

He once had to borrow money from me and other friends because he lost his entire month's budget gambling in an underground casino.

He also participates in underground races and does a lot of base jumping. We used to do interventions, but he never takes us seriously. He keeps saying that he doesn't feel alive and these things that he does are his way to feel alive.

He just went away one day and none of us heard from him again. I sincerely hope that he's doing okay.

As I said, it's normal to take risks but it's only good if you have taken the time to think about it and you're not unnecessarily risking your life or property.

I believe that to succeed in life, a person needs to take certain risks but these risks should be manageable calculated risks.

When you find yourself betting too much for a relatively small amount of gain or if you stop caring whether you lose a lot just for the thrill of taking a risk then you have a problem.

People who don't love themselves don't care about what they are putting on the line and risk everything for small, irrational potential gains.

6) You Have Self-Destructive Behaviors

Do you have any behaviors that cause you harm? Anything that gives you short-term pleasure at the cost of harming yourself or the people you care about may be considered self-destructive behaviors.

Just the fact that you are deliberately harming yourself means that you don't love yourself enough. You're supposed to take care of yourself but instead, you hurt yourself.

You settle for a relatively small and short-term relief even if you already know that it's not going to be good for you in the long run.

You keep smoking even if you already know that you risk getting lung cancer. You drink excessively and sometimes use it as an excuse for bad behavior.

You do a lot of drugs and take large doses in an attempt to maximize the pleasure you'll feel even if you could die from an overdose.

You practice unsafe, unprotected sex with prostitutes or partners with questionable backgrounds.

It could also be that maybe you're not aware that you're sabotaging yourself or simply don't notice the damage you're doing because you don't take time to consider your actions and what the consequences are for such actions.

The worst thing is when you don't even listen to the people who care about you anymore and you think that they're just holding you back. You stopped thinking of consequences and just go for whatever feels good at the time.

7) You're Too Needy

Everyone craves attention one way or another. We each have the desire to be appreciated and we all need to be needed.

It's just how we all are. We're social creatures that need affirmation and appreciation from others. That's why we all try to express ourselves in interesting ways like showing off our talents or augmenting our features with makeup and fashion.

The problem is when the attention-seeking makes you too clingy or overbearing.

When you constantly feel the need for affirmation and the approval of other people and go to great lengths to get the attention you seek, it tends to drive people away instead of drawing them closer.

Sometimes, you give away so much of yourself just to gain the approval of others.

You have such a low opinion of your worth that you no longer have standards and just go for anything that seems to be within reach especially when it comes to your relationships.

Another way this happens is when you put too much value on others that you put them on a pedestal and worship them. You feel a strong need to earn their approval that you're willing to do just about anything for them, even if it causes you harm.

You get serious in your relationships too quickly and you feel the need to lock the other person in right away.

You feel the need to be with them every minute and you call or text them excessively and when they don't answer you immediately freak out. You keep checking your phone for a reply and you tend to imagine a lot of worst-case scenarios on why they aren't answering you without even taking into consideration the fact that they might be busy with something.

8) You're Too Afraid to Make Mistakes

Like I said earlier, it's okay to make the occasional mistake. You're only human after all, and there are things that you miss or overlook.

Being afraid of making a mistake is also natural, I mean who likes screwing upright? When you find yourself continually overthinking every little thing and get paralysis by analysis, then it's time to consider that you may have a problem.

You're so scared of being ridiculed that you don't share your opinions even when asked about it. You go along with whatever other people tell you to do, and you don't complain even if you're suffering because you're afraid that doing your own thing is an even bigger mistake. You let other people choose for you all the time, ranging from the simplest thing like picking ice cream flavors to major ones like picking a car model.

When you make decisions, you can't help but second-guess and wonder if you can still take it back. Whenever you're faced with a choice, you try to analyze every detail and you try to predict everything that could go wrong until you end up having to unnecessarily delay or try to get someone else to choose for you.

You're afraid of taking responsibility for any negative consequences of your choices that you make everything into a democratic process where you ask for everyone's opinions and go with whatever choice has more votes, even if inside your head, you know that it's not the best course of action.

Conclusion

There comes a time when you need to trust yourself. You dictate how happy your life will be. If you get to the point of self-acceptance and love, everything else falls into place.

Look around you at confident people. They accept who they are and many people can do this from a very young age. Those with secure backgrounds and who grow up with parents who can nurture them may never experience negative feelings about themselves.

They may take for granted that everyone feels as they do.

However, life isn't that simplistic. In a way, you have been through the worst stage of your life and have accepted that you need to do something about self-love.

If you have done all of the exercises in this book, you will already feel better about yourself and will have recovered from feeling negative.

Negativity may have been the result of many years of self-criticism so your positive approach to life from now on is necessary to override all of the negativity you have accepted as part of your life.

You can look at yourself in the mirror and see your true self.

You are compassionate and kind and don't resort to things that diminish who you are. You know that negative emotions don't help you to present yourself in a way that others accept easily.

You also know that the responsibility for who you are is yours and no one else.

Taking that responsibility in hand and realizing it's yours is a step in the right direction because your change of attitude means that you can cope with other people's negativity levels without making them rub off on you.

With all of the world in turmoil and with the pressures of life in the twenty-first century, your self-acceptance and love is the first turning point in your life that helps you to succeed and be happy. Stand on each stepping stone and don't be afraid of the next. The water isn't deep enough to drown you.

Yes, sometimes you get your feet wet, but that's a natural progression and you learn from each mistake in life to tread more carefully in the future.

You are a very valuable human being with an entitlement to opinions of your own. You don't have to bow to the opinions of others.

We have taught you how to deal with relationships and how to make relationships work for you.

Your new positive attitude will help you to make friends. The fact that you have been on this journey of discovery means that you can see yourself as complete and don't need someone else to prop up who you are.

That's wonderful news. Mr. or Mrs. Right won't be looking for broken people. They will be looking for whole people whose love for themselves allows them freedom of expression and positivity.

You need to remember that if you continue to display yourself as "broken" no one can fix you. You have to do it yourself.

This book gives you all of the secrets and yes, it can be done within 30 days. That 30 day gives you a point of reference and if you have not yet tried and tested the theories within this book, your thirty days begins now.

It is hoped that you come out of the other side of your negativity with strong self-love.

People who love themselves don't leave themselves open to abuse. They encourage healthy giving relationships.

They present themselves as balanced and happy and are capable of much more than they give themselves credit for.

Welcome to the world of complete people.

page intentionally left blank

CPSIA information can be obtained
at www.ICGtesting.com
Printed in the USA
BVHW041054080321
601999BV00006B/372